My Salads To You

By
Donia Craig Dickerson

Best wishes,

Donia Dickerson

Spring 2011

For Beth —
Thank you, thank you for
all the courtesies and kindnesses

Westview Publishing Co., Inc. – Nashville, Tennessee

you always extend to me —
with affection —
Donia Dickerson

Fall 2011

First Edition published 1985
Second Edition published 2005

Printed in the United States of America on acid-free paper

ISBN 0-9764940-7-8

Page and cover layout by Westview Publishing Co., Inc.

Westview Publishing Co., Inc.
8120 Sawyer Brown Road, Suite 107
PO Box 210183
Nashville, TN 37221
westviewpublishing.com

To Buford

CONTENTS

FOREWORD

As one who is fumble-fingered in the kitchen and therefore relies on the fruits (or salads) of other people's culinary efforts, I'm more likely to think of salad in terms of Shakespeare's Cleopatra who laughingly passed off her fickleness in love as due to "My salad days, when I was green in judgment, cold in blood." Or to take a critic's pleasure in the Spanish proverb that states the requisites for a good salad: A spendthrift for oil, a miser for vinegar, a counselor for salt, and a madman to stir it all up. I visualize that as a comedy for the Stooges (Four instead of Three), with all that dramatic action boiling about in full fury on the stage!

Being kitchen-shy doesn't mean a lack of pleasure in these mixes of garden provender, or in reading about them either. Here's a different sort of cook book, written with wit and a light touch, enjoyable on its own terms and calculated to send an admitted non-cook out to find a pepper mill and a ring mold, some basil and fresh spinach, and a bit of brandy for the mayonnaise. If Cleopatra could share such salads, her heart would grow warm and she would have to find another metaphor to explain the fitfulness of her affections.

Clara Hieronymus
Art and Theater Critic (retired)
The Tennessean

INTRODUCTION

Welcome to my salad world! May this book provide you with recipes often to be enjoyed. But, more importantly, may it enhance an already vivid imagination, add to your already superb inventory of ideas in the salad category, or happily join your other favorite cook books on a shelf which never collects dust.

The salad category was chosen for my entry into this already saturated market because the salad gives license to creativity. An unabashed lover of art, who cannot paint my name, I find that the creative juices freely flow with each dash—each drop—and that each ingredient adds to the salad. Personally, I have to follow recipes for cakes, cookies, and pies. I stick to the rules for proportions for soufflés, quiches, sauces, etc., adding my ideas about the seasonings. But a good salad, one fit for kings, can be prepared and served with only garden fresh greens, fine olive oil, wine vinegar, salt and freshly ground black pepper. So, "Go with your flow!"

Please understand and enjoy the freedom with which this book has been compiled and printed. There is probably not a single recipe in *My Salads To You* that has not already been printed in some form or fashion. If these ideas are new to you, good for me! Vicarious enjoyment will be my reward.

You will observe that many salads are not so much omitted, as they are simply without a recipe. For example, freshly grated Parmesan cheese, or crumbled blue cheese, usually appear on my salads of mixed greens with vinegar and oil. Some salad lovers add chopped green onions or freshly snipped herbs. There is no Chef Salad included. A Chef Salad is your creation; diced ham, chicken, cheese, quartered hard-cooked eggs, tomato wedges, croutons—whatever. You may prefer the addition of radishes, cucumbers, bell peppers or carrots.

A marinated vegetable salad plate is not included. There is no recipe. Simply marinate any combination of vegetables such as artichoke hearts, whole green beans, cherry tomatoes, beets, baby carrots, etc. Arrange your combination on lettuce leaves and let your guests choose their favorites.

But, I do include what my favorite late columnist titled "Strictly Personal Prejudices." Thoughts about congealed salads, choice of salad greens, tomatoes out of season, etc., are found elsewhere. Let us take a few minutes to examine the "whys and why nots" of certain items. Take, for example, the continued call for "freshly ground black or white pepper." Maybe you cannot tell the difference. I argue that there is no comparison. If nothing else, there is something therapeutic in those hand-ground specks that fall on the greens. They may be tantamount to sugar pills for the hypochondriac, but they work.

To me, garlic salt is a "no-no." Cheating in Cream Cheese Balls goes unnoticed; however, dried onion flakes may be substituted to save time. Buy croutons if you must. "Store bought" is better than "no bought." As to herbs, of course fresh herbs are more desirable. Would that I had a greenhouse. A sunny kitchen window works for some. If you do not have a greenhouse, suffer with the rest of us. Use dried herbs, and put your window herbs outside after Blackberry Winter. Paprika and parsley are not repeatedly mentioned. Do not overdo the use of paprika—respect its taste, enjoy its colour, and use it for unusual effects. Obviously, cottage cheese, chicken, turkey, and seafood salads, deviled eggs, potato salad, etc., call for paprika. An unappealing contrast would be about as effective as "red chorine," for colour influences the mind far more than we realize.

Parsley sprigs should accent every salad plate. Parsley freshens the breath and is very high in potassium. Further, watercress should grace the more elegant salads. Somehow, watercress does not belong with a potato salad plate as much as a first course of Eggs En Gelée. But then, I put watercress on my breakfast plate if I am having broiled fish or fried tomatoes. There is no rule. The only one I adhere to is to beg, borrow or steal this culinary jewel. Keep watercress separate in the refrigerator. For garnish, shake necessary amount in a bag with equal amounts of salt and pepper just before serving.

Chutney is used in these recipes. I cannot imagine not making your own chutney. It is so easy to make and is not just for curried dishes. Do not hesitate to use "store bought" curry, however. There are some good brands. A pear or peach chutney goes nicely with the Pineapple Chutney Salad and with mayonnaise for artichokes. But, as in all things worthwhile, your own is far superior.

As to "hints and tricks," I hesitated to burden you with a trite list so often found in some cook books. If you use this book. you already have your own tricks. for this is not a text for "Cooking 101-A." Further, I have a habit of presuming that everyone knows the basics in cooking and fear talking down to people when I teach. When in doubt, always refer to your favorite basic cook book.

And so, in closing, whoever you are and wherever you may be, I wish you a very happy culinary life. Bon appétit to all you love and to you.

Donia Craig Dickerson

SALADS

APRICOT SALAD
Serves 8

1 Package lemon gelatin
1 ½ Cups apricot nectar
3 Tablespoons lemon juice
Boston or Bibb lettuce

1/3 Cup orange juice
1 4-ounce package cream
  cheese
1 Cup chopped pecans

Dissolve gelatin with boiling apricot nectar, orange and lemon juice. Stir until dissolved. Pour into individual molds or a ring mold and refrigerate. When the salad has become slightly congealed, place the cream cheese balls, which have been rolled in pecans, in the center. Un-mold on Boston or Bibb lettuce and serve with mayonnaise.

ARTICHOKES

I wish artichoke came before apricot in the alphabet because this one of a kind and acquired-taste jewel, which is habit forming, would have been my opening item!

Observe the artichoke eater—if you have time to look up. He pulls off each leaf carefully, frantically dips it into the chosen sauce, looks at it as though God had monogramed his initials on it, and scrapes the edible part into his mouth with sensuous pleasure; and, at the bottom is indeed his "golden egg."

Soak fresh artichokes in kosher salt; drain and boil covered until the leaves easily pull off— forty-five minutes to one hour. Add a celery stalk and lemon quarter, squeezed, to the water. Drain upside down and chill or serve immediately.

For parties, trim the leaves, remove the choke, gently pull the leaves open and serve with the filling in the center.

15

ARTICHOKES WITH:

Lemon Butter

Allow ½ cup drawn butter per artichoke. Serve hot as a first course with lemon quarters on the plate.

Mayonnaise

Same as above. Serve hot or cold as a first course.

Stuff With

Seafood salad, scallop salad, chicken or turkey salad. Serve as a main luncheon course.

Fill With

Chutney, celery or dill mayonnaise. Serve as a first course.

Note: An "Artichoke Tasting Cocktail Party" is , great fun. Label the fillings with place card holders. This is messy but no one minds the sight of the discarded leaves. Remember to have several forks and a knife at each artichoke plate for the prize.

AVOCADOS

An avocado is not an avocado by any other name! Here in Nashville, we can generally find the large, bright green Florida variety and the summer, darker green, California ones. Although some people are quite fussy about their selection of this glorious fruit, I maintain that this is one time size wins out over taste and texture. Obviously, one is not going to serve ½ avocado of the large variety to an individual as a first course! But the large ones are a must for slicing through the middle as a base for a tomato aspic salad.

Avocados may be purchased while they are firm, placed in a fruit ripener or drawer; and, in two to three days, stored in the refrigerator to be used that day. If you use only part of an avocado, leave the seed in tact, squeeze lemon juice over the cut part and wrap tightly in foil. If selecting an avocado for use that day, be sure it is not bruised or overripe. Avocados are best when barely tender to thumb pressure. The ways to serve avocado halves are unending. Here is a good list to be augmented by your imagination.

Note: Start your avocado plant! Wash the avocado seed in warm water and cut off the tip of the small end. Place three toothpicks in the top half and support the seed in a glass of warm water. When the leaves and roots appear, plant in rich soil in a clay pot. After four or five leaves appear, cut back in half. Your avocado tree will want sunshine and a lot of water. If your seed fails to sprout, cut it up and feed it to other houseplants. Children love to try this.

AVOCADOS FILLED WITH:

BACON, TOMATO, AND ARTICHOKE
Serves 4

2 Avocados
2 Artichoke hearts, chopped
½ Cup mayonnaise
2 Medium tomatoes
4 Strips bacon, crumbled
1 Green onion

Salt and freshly ground white
   pepper to taste
Dash cayenne
Paprika
Boston or Bibb lettuce

Peel, seed, chop and drain tomatoes. Combine all ingredients and chill well. Fill peeled avocado halves with mixture and top with mayonnaise sprinkled with paprika. Serve on a bed of lettuce with cheese dreams or open-faced cucumber sandwiches.

CHICKEN OR TURKEY SALAD
Fills 2 Halves

1 Avocado	Mayonnaise
Chicken or turkey salad	Paprika
Basic Dressing	Boston or Bibb lettuce

Fill avocado halves with ~ cup chicken or turkey salad. Top with mayonnaise and sprinkle with paprika. Serve on a bed of lettuce which has been tossed with BASIC DRESSING. Garnish with hard-cooked egg quarters, tomato quarters and one or two sweet-sour pickles.

CREAM CHEESE BALLS

Cream cheese	Grapefruit and orange
BASIC DRESSING	sections
Boston or Bibb lettuce	Rosemary leaves
	Paprika

In peeled avocado halves, place one or two cream cheese balls and fill the rest of the cavity with BASIC DRESSING. Serve on lettuce and sprinkle with paprika. Surround with grapefruit and orange sections which have been sprinkled with rosemary leaves. Serve with watercress sandwiches.

CREAM CHEESE AND CAVIAR
Serves 4

2 Avocados	1 Teaspoon onion juice
1 8-ounce package cream cheese	1 Small jar black caviar
	Lemon wedges
2 Tablespoons mayonnaise	Boston or Bibb lettuce
2 Tablespoons vodka	

Have cream cheese at room temperature. Blend well with mayonnaise and onion juice until smooth. Add the vodka, blend and fill peeled avocado halves with mixture. Top with caviar and serve on Boston or Bibb lettuce with lemon wedges. This combination is mouth watering even before you taste. This may be served with chilled white wine as a first course.

LEMON JUICE AND OIL
Serves 2

1 Avocado	Salt and white pepper to taste
Olive Oil	Boston or Bibb lettuce
1 Large lemon quartered	

Do not peel avocado. Cut in half, remove seed and place on lettuce. Fill cavity 2/3 full with oil and place lemon quarters on the side. Pass salt and pepper. Some people think an avocado served any other way "gilds the lily."

SEVICHE

Avocados
Seviche
Boston or Bibb lettuce

Fill desired number of peeled avocado halves with 1/3 cup Seviche. Place in a chilled bowl lined with Boston lettuce and serve as a first course. Serve with 2 ounces vodka poured over crushed ice. This, in addition to being delicious, is a "conversation piece" as so few people serve Seviche.

SCALLOP OR SEA FOOD SALAD

Avocados	Basic Dressing
Scallop or seafood salad	Boston or Bibb lettuce
Mayonnaise	Paprika

Fill desired number of avocado halves with 1/3 to 1/2 cup scallop Or seafood salad. Top with mayonnaise, sprinkle with paprika and serve on a bed of lettuce that has been tossed with Basic Dressing.

Garnish with hard-cooked egg quarters, tomato wedges and 1 or 2 sweet-sour pickles and a lemon wedge.

SOUR CREAM AND CAVIAR
Serves 4

2 Avocados	¼ Teaspoon salt
1 Small carton sour cream	¼ Teaspoon white pepper
1 Small jar red caviar	Lemon wedges
1 Tablespoon white wine	Boston or Bibb lettuce

Mix sour cream, white wine, salt and pepper. Fill peeled avocado halves with the mixture, top with caviar and serve on lettuce with lemon wedges. Serve with white wine for a perfect first course.

AVOCADO-TOMATO ASPIC RING
Serves 8-10

For Avocado-Tomato Aspic Ring, prepare half of the following receipes for Tomato Aspic and Avocado Rings.

Fill an oiled ring mold with the avocado mix and let it set. Then pour in the tomato aspic, slightly set, and chill at least three hours.

Unmold on Boston or Bibb lettuce and fill the center with three cups chicken or shrimp salad. Garnish with hard-cooked eggs and marinated fresh asparagus.

This salad served with cheese dreams is a perfect
and easy to serve luncheon delight.

TOMATO ASPIC
Serves 8-10

4 Cups tomato juice
1 Onion, cut in half
4 Ribs celery and leaves,
  chopped
1 Teaspoon sugar
3 Tablespoons lemon juice
1 Bay leaf
1 Tablespoon Worcestershire
  sauce

2 ½ Tablespoons unseasoned
  gelatin
½ Cup cold water
Spinach or mixed lettuce
Desired Filling
Salt and freshly ground white
  pepper to taste

Soak the gelatin in the cold water. Combine all ingredients in a
saucepan and simmer for at least thirty minutes. Generously season
the aspic as chilling reduces the flavor. Strain into a bowl and stir
in the gelatin. Pour into well-oiled 1 ½ quart ring mold. Chill.

Unmold on a bed of spinach or mixed lettuce which has been
lightly tossed with Basic Dressing. Fill the center with chicken or
turkey salad, seafood salad or cottage cheese which has been
highly seasoned with horseradish and mayonnaise. Or fill
the center with citrus slices and surround the mold with avocado
slices and marinated artichoke halves.

AVOCADO RING
Serves 8-10

1 Cup ripe avocado, mashed
1 Envelope unseasoned
  gelatin
¼ Cup vermouth or white
  wine
1 Cup chicken stock
2 Tablespoons lemon juice
½ Cup sour cream
½ Cup mayonnaise

Salt and freshly ground white
  pepper to taste
Dash cayenne
6 Drops Tabasco sauce
Watercress or mixed lettuce
Basic Dressing
Grapefruit and orange
  sections

21

Soak the gelatin in the vermouth. Add boiling stock and mix well. Put the avocado in the blender with the lemon juice and puree. Mix all ingredients until smooth. Pour into an oiled, 1 ½ quart ring mold, or 6 individual molds, and chill several hours.

Unmold on a bed of mixed lettuce or watercress, which has been tossed with Basic Dressing, and fill the center with grapefruit and orange sections. Top with Pomegranate or Poppy Seed dressing.

BEET SALAD

Beets
Onions (Vidalia spring, if possible)
Basic Dressing
Horseradish (freshly grated, if possible)
Mayonnaise
Mixed greens

Marinate separately equal parts sliced, fresh beets (barely cooked) and sliced onions in Basic Dressing for several hours. Alternate desired number on mixed greens. Top each serving with mayonnaise which has been highly seasoned with horseradish.

CONGEALED BROCCOLI SALAD RING I
Serves 6-8

1 Package unflavored gelatin
1 Cup chicken stock
½ Cup chicken stock
2 Tablespoons mayonnaise
3 Dashes Tabasco
Dash crushed red pepper
Dash Worcestershire sauce
Pinch grated, whole nutmeg

Salt and freshly ground white pepper to taste
1 Medium bunch fresh broccoli (Use stalks, leaves and flowerets)
¾ Cup mayonnaise
Boston or Bibb lettuce

Sprinkle gelatin on ½ cup chicken stock. Heat 1 cup chicken stock. Add to gelatin mixture along with all other ingredients. Chop broccoli finely and combine with the gelatin mixture. Pour into ring mold which has been oiled. Chill until firm.

Unmold on a bed of Boston or Bibb lettuce and fill the center with mayonnaise.

Variation: Fill center with cauliflower and broccoli flowerets which have been marinated in Basic Dressing and chilled.

Note: Boil the cauliflower core and tough broccoli Stalks. Drain and freeze for vegetable soup or liquid for cheese sauce for vegetables.

BROCCOLI RING II
Serves 6-8

2 Packages frozen chopped broccoli
4 Hard cooked eggs, chopped
¾ Cup mayonnaise
1 Package unflavored gelatin
2 Tablespoons lemon juice or white wine
4 Tablespoons Worcestershire sauce
1 Can condensed consomme
3 Drops Tabasco sauce
Boston or Bibb lettuce

Sprinkle gelatin in ¼ cup cold water. Add heated consomme and stir until dissolved. Add all other ingredients; the broccoli and eggs last. Pour into an oiled ring mold. Unmold on lettuce and fill the center with mayonnaise.

This salad ring is good for large parties as it holds well and men like it, unlike most "lady luncheon salads."

CAESAR SALAD

Serves 8-10

3 Medium heads Romaine
2 Peeled cloves garlic,
    quartered
2/3 Cup salad oil
2 Cups croutons
½ Cup grated Parmesan
    cheese
½ Teaspoon salt

¼ Teaspoon freshly grated
    pepper
1 Raw egg or 1 egg coddled
    one minute
1 Teaspoon Worcestershire
    sauce
3 Tablespoons lemon juice

Note: Omit garlic if you keep garlic oil on hand. Use 2/3 cup garlic oil. Some versions call for ¼ cup crumbled blue cheese.

Let garlic stand in oil at kitchen temperature for several hours and remove. Tear the lettuce into pieces. In a large salad bowl, mix the lettuce, croutons, optional blue cheese, salt and pepper, vinegar and oil. Crack the raw or coddled egg over the salad, pour the Worcestershire sauce and lemon juice over the egg, and toss again. Serve at once.

You may question the lack of anchovies. I feel that this is "neither the time nor place!"

CHICKEN OR TURKEY SALAD

Diced chicken or turkey
Diced celery, some leaves
    also
White pepper
Paprika

Mayonnaise
Lemon juice
Dash curry powder, optional
Boston or Bibb lettuce

I simply can not bring myself to print an actual recipe for chicken or turkey salad. Some people would think of using nothing but white meat. I use all the chicken or turkey for sandwiches and only white meat for stuffing avocados, artichokes or tomatoes.

For each cup of meat, use ½ cup celery, 1 tablespoon of freshly squeezed lemon juice. Bind with mayonnaise. I am very generous with my amount of mayonnaise for stuffing--very light for sandwiches.

The main thing is to be heavy on white pepper. Season your chicken salad until it is absolutely perfect--you will know.

CHICKEN SALAD IN CANTALOUPE RINGS
Serves 6

3 Cups chicken salad
6 Cantaloupe rings cut ½ inch
   thick

1 Cup slivered almonds,
   toasted
1 Cup seedless green grapes
Watercress or mixed greens

Combine chicken salad, grapes and almonds. Serve in cantaloupe rings on a bed of watercress of mixed greens. Top with mayonnaise, thinned with sherry to taste. This combination is exotic.

CHICKEN SALAD RING
Serves 8-10

2 Envelopes unflavored
   gelatin
2 Cups mayonnaise
2 Cups chicken stock
¼ Cup cold water
6 Cups diced chicken

2 Cups diced celery
¼ Cup lemon juice
Salt and freshly ground white
   pepper to taste
Dash curry powder, optional
Mixed greens

Soften gelatin in cold water and dissolve in hot chicken stock. Cool. Combine remaining ingredients, adding gelatin last. Pour into oiled mold and chill. Unmold on a bed of mixed greens.

Fill the center with cantaloupe balls with poppy seed dressing or mayonnaise mixed with chopped walnuts or slivered almonds. This ring mold is very elegant and rather uncommon.

CHILI RING FOR SEAFOOD SALAD

1 Cup chili sauce
1 Envelope gelatin
½ Cup cold water
1 Cup whipping cream
1 4-ounce package of cream
   cheese
1 Cup mayonnaise

Horseradish to taste
Salt and freshly ground
   pepper to taste
Tabasco sauce to taste
Desired filling
Deviled eggs
Watercress or mixed lettuce

Heat chili sauce to the boiling point. Pour over gelatin and stir. Add the cream cheese and mix until smooth. When cool, blend in other ingredients and pour into a 1 ½ quart ring mold. When chilled, unmold on a bed of lettuce and fill the center with crab or shrimp salad. Garnish with deviled eggs and watercress or mixed lettuce.

CITRUS, CHEESE BALLS, AVOCADO AND ARTICHOKE HEARTS

Arrange equal parts grapefruit, orange and avocado sections on a bed of mixed greens, Boston or Bibb lettuce. On each plate add one cheese ball and one artichoke heart stuffed with blue cheese. Serve with either orange mayonnaise or poppy seed dressing. Generally, one grapefruit, orange, and avocado will serve four.

CITRUS SALAD II
Serves 6

Cream Cheese Ring recipe	2 Ripe avocados
Grapefruit	1 Can artichoke hearts
Oranges	Mixed greens

On beds of mixed greens, unmold individual cream cheese ring molds. On the outside, surround with avocado slices. Fill the center with grapefruit and orange slices. Top the center with an artichoke heart or with a mound of chopped artichoke. Top with 2 to 3 tablespoons Poppy Seed Dressing. Serve as a first course or as a luncheon salad with an assortment of watercress, cucumber, and chicken salad sandwiches.

COLD MEAT SALAD PLATE

Thinly sliced cold beef, veal, chicken or turkey cut into julienne strips	Hard-cooked eggs
	Tomatoes
	Boston or Bibb lettuce
Red wine vinegar	Red onion rings
Olive oil	Dijon mustard
French Potato Salad	Mayonnaise

Marinate any of the left-over meat and onion rings in vinegar and oil. Mound the meat and onion rings on a plate of lettuce, surround it with potato salad, tomato quarters, and halved hard-cooked eggs. Pass mustard or mayonnaise.

For sliced ham, Canadian bacon, or pork roast, marinate the meat and onion rings in sherry and pass chutney mayonnaise.

Note: There are no set proportions for a cold plate like this, but a good rule of thumb is; ½ cup meat, 2 or 3 onion rings barely covered with half vinegar and half oil, and ½ cup potato salad per person.

COTTAGE CHEESE

Mix cottage cheese with mayonnaise, chopped green onions, tops included, salt and freshly ground white pepper, paprika, and a dash of cayenne. Chill well.

COTTAGE CHEESE RING

1 Pint cottage cheese, room temperature
1 8-ounce package cream cheese
1 Small bunch green onions
½ Cup mayonnaise
1 Envelope unflavored gelatin
1 Tablespoon cold water
1 Tablespoon boiling water
Peeled, diced tomatoes
Salt and freshly ground white pepper to taste
Paprika
Mixed salad greens
Fresh or dried basil

Cream the cream cheese with the mayonnaise until smooth. Sprinkle the gelatin on the water, and dissolve it with boiling water. Chop the onions, tops included, and mix all ingredients. Season well and pour into an oiled ring mold. Chill. Unmold on a bed of lettuce. sprinkle with paprika, and fill the center with peeled, diced tomatoes which have been marinated in Basic Dressing. Garnish with fresh basil leaves.

COUNTRY SALAD
Serves 1

½ Hard-cooked egg, grated
1 Slice bacon, cooked and crumbled
Mixed greens
Salt and freshly ground black pepper to taste
1-2 Tablespoons Standard Dressing to taste

Mix together and serve at once with a scoop of cottage cheese in the center.

Nashvillians will remember this served by wonderful Betty at Moon Drug Store.

CRAB MEAT SALAD
Serves 6

2 Pounds fresh, lump crab meat

2 Medium white onions, finely chopped

½ Pint salad oil

Less than ½ pint cider vinegar

1 Cup ice water

Salt and freshly ground white pepper to taste

Mixed greens

Combine all ingredients except ice water. Sprinkle with salt and pepper. Add ice water, cover in air tight container, and chill for two to twelve hours. Serve with a slotted spoon onto the mixed greens.

This is the famous recipe from Bayley's Restaurant in Mobile, Alabama, as nearly as I can duplicate it.

CREAM CHEESE RING
Serves 8-10

2 4-ounce packages cream cheese

1 Cup whipping cream

½ Cup mayonnaise

2 Teaspoons grated onion

½ Teaspoon salt

6 Drops Tabasco

¼ Teaspoon Worcestershire Sauce

1 Package unflavored gelatin

¼ Cup cold water

Boston or Bibb lettuce

Sprinkle the gelatin over the cold water. In the top of a double boiler, melt all the ingredients. Mix and beat well. Add the dissolved gelatin and mix well.

Pour into a well-greased ring mold and chill until firm. Unmold on a bed of lettuce on a chilled plate, and fill the center with a small container of Poppy Seed or Pomegranate Dressing.

Surround the ring with alternating layers of grapefruit and orange sections, avocado slices or marinated artichoke hearts. Or fill the center with the fruit, surround with the avocado and artichoke hearts and serve the dressing on the side.

CUCUMBER MOUSSE
Serves 6

3 Cucumbers
1 Teaspoon Worcestershire
  Sauce
½ Teaspoon salt
½ Cup mayonnaise
½ Cup whipping cream,
  whipped
1 ½ Envelopes gelatin

1 Teaspoon grated onion
3 Tablespoons white wine or
  cold water
2 Teaspoons hot lemon juice
Freshly ground white pepper
  to taste
Watercress

Grate the cucumber and drain in a colander. Soften the gelatin in the wine and dissolve in hot lemon juice.

Combine all ingredients, fold in the whipped cream, and chill in a fish mold (or six individual molds). Unmold on a bed of watercress, decorate the top of the mold with sliced cucumbers which have been marinated in Basic Dressing and sprinkled with chives, or unmold on tomato slices. Fill the center of the mold with drained, thinly sliced cucumbers and top with mayonnaise.

Note: You must double this recipe in order to fill a decorative fish mold. In the summer, when cucumbers are fresh and not those horrible waxed things, season accordingly to retain good cucumber taste. In the wintertime, season heavily with white pepper.

CUCUMBER SALAD

Serves 6

3 Cucumbers
1 Tablespoon salt
2 Green onions
½ Teaspoon white pepper

1/3 Cup white wine vinegar
1/3 Cup sour cream
Chervil, chives or parsley
Mixed greens

Peel the cucumbers, slice very thinly, sprinkle with salt, and let stand for 30 minutes to one hour. Drain.

Combine all the ingredients and chill for several hours.

Serve on a bed of mixed greens and top with chopped chives, chervil, or parsley.

CUCUMBER, VEAL, AND WATERCRESS SALAD

Cold roast veal (¼ pound per serving)
Cucumbers (¼ pound per serving)
Watercress (Boston or Bibb lettuce if not in season)
Salt and freshly ground white pepper to taste
Dill croutons
White wine

Cut into julienne strips equal parts of roast veal and unpeeled cucumbers. Pepper the veal generously and marinate in white wine for at least two hours.

On a bed of watercress, layer the veal first, then the cucumbers. Sprinkle with dill croutons and top with lime mayonnaise.

This salad is an exciting "first taste" for most people.

The refrain of that "ABC. .." hit song, recorded by every elementary school teacher in America, "Now, I've Sung My ABC's, Tell Me What You Think Of Me," rang through my head as I filed away *My Salads To You*. Comes now my only "D" and it is not a salad.

The irreplaceable and irresistible "Deviled Egg" cuts a wide swath. It has probably gone on more picnics. into more lunch boxes. box suppers. etc., than any other culinary item. It has danced at every Charity Ball (topped with caviar. of course), graced every buffet table, and can probably boast 100% attendance in every cafeteria type restaurant line that was ever walked through. My special thanks go to whoever split open that first hard-cooked oval joy and "stuffed it."

DEVILED EGGS

Shell the eggs, cut them in halves, remove the yolks, and mash with a fork very finely. Combine with just enough mayonnaise to make a smooth paste. Be careful, as one quick dump too many can make the filling runny. Season with salt, dry mustard, paprika and white pepper to taste. Top with chopped parsley.

Variations for Garnish

The permutations and combinations of seasonings for Deviled Eggs are endless--use your imagination. There are no measurements; each is "to taste." On eggs sprinkle the following to accompany:

Chicken Salad -Poultry seasoning, capers, orange or lime marmalade
Cold Meat Platter -Rosemary or chutney with lamb, sage or thyme with pork, horseradish with roast beef
Cucumber Mousse -Dill weed, dill seed, or chives
Potato Salad - Mix in sweet relish or chopped green onions.
Seafood Salads -Red or black caviar
Tomato Aspic Ring -Basil leaves

If you prefer to surround your salad plates with hard-cooked eggs, always, at least, sprinkle them with paprika. Follow the above suggestions and never serve either deviled or hard-cooked halves without a sprig of parsley in the center.

EGGS EN GELÉE I
Serves 6

Eggs in aspic are served on a bed of lettuce as a first course, a luncheon dish, or around cold meat slices at a buffet. Traditionally, poached eggs are used, but a deviled egg half, unmolded egg side up in the mold, is equally delicious.

6 Poached eggs, trimmed and
  cooled
12 Fresh tarragon leaves or
  12 leaves from a tarragon
  vinegar bottle
1 Package unflavored gelatin
1 Cup canned chicken broth
  or
1 Cup homemade chicken
  stock

½ Cup cold chicken stock or
  broth
½ Teaspoon sugar
½ Teaspoon salt
1/8 Cup tarragon vinegar
1 Small jar red or black
caviar
¼ Cup mayonnaise
¼ Cup sour cream
1/8 Cup lemon juice

Sprinkle gelatin on cold stock or broth. Heat remaining ingredients and combine with gelatin. Pour a small amount in the bottom of six individual ramekins or molds, and refrigerate until the gelatin begins to set. Place the tarragon leaves in the design of an 'X.' When the leaves are firmly set, place an egg in each mold and cover with the remaining mixture. Refrigerate until congealed Unmold on a bed of lettuce and top with mayonnaise and sour cream mixed. Sprinkle with caviar and serve with white wine.

EGGS EN GELÉE II
Serves 6

The French would not approve, but the following version is delicious.

3 Eggs, hard cooked
2 Green onions, chopped
2 Tablespoons mayonnaise
Salt and freshly ground white pepper to taste
1 Small jar red or black caviar
¼ Cup mayonnaise
¼ Cup sour cream

Make gelatin according to Eggs En Gelée I. Prepare the molds or ramekins the same way. Half the eggs lengthwise, remove the yolks and mash with a fork until fluffy. Add the mayonnaise and green onions and season well.

Place one half egg, stuffed side up, in the mold and cover with the gelatin mixture. Refrigerate until congealed.

Top with ¼ cup mayonnaise, ¼ cup sour cream, and sprinkle with caviar.

Variation: Double the recipe and fill a ring mold with whole stuffed eggs. In between each egg, set fresh sprigs of snipped dill and parsley. Unmold on a bed of lettuce. Fill the center with mayonnaise and sour cream mixture and top with caviar.

This beautiful aspic, a bottle of white wine, cucumber and watercress sandwiches make a memory luncheon on the terrace.

FAUCON SALAD

Serves 1

I believe I know where this fabulous combination originated, but I am afraid to tell. The only place I have seen it on the menu is the Belle Meade Country Club here in Nashville. This is the only time I suggest iceberg lettuce--it is a must.

For each individual salad bowl:

1 Strip bacon crumbled
½ Grated egg
¼ Cup combination mayonnaise and blue cheese to taste
Combination bibb and iceberg lettuce--mostly iceberg

Break the lettuce into fairly large pieces. A knife is used with this salad. In the center, place the mayonnaise, add the bacon, and grate the egg over the center. A double Faucon Salad is a luncheon meal; a single is perfect with any sandwich choice for luncheon.

FRUIT SALAD PLATE

Here again, there is no set rule for this summer delight. On a bed of mixed lettuce, use the desired amount of any fruit of the season, diced, sliced, whatever. Place a small serving in a crystal container of mint sherbet and pass Poppy Seed Dressing. Serve cream cheese and date nut bread sandwiches and you will please your guests greatly.

Note: Blueberries, raspberries, or blackberries give a good visual accent to the usual peaches, plums, pears, etc. I do not push bananas on this plate.

For a pretty center piece for this plate, place a cantaloupe ring topped with a cream cheese ball mixed with guava or wine jelly. Serve with Pomegranate Dressing.

GUACAMOLE
Serves 6

3 Large avocados
2 Tablespoons lemon juice
1 Tablespoon lime juice
¼ Teaspoon chili powder
1/3 Cup mayonnaise
2 Tablespoons grated onion
1 Clove crushed garlic

1 Tablespoon Basic Dressing
Few drops Tabasco
Generous dash of cracked red
  pepper
Salt and freshly ground white
  pepper to taste

Combine all ingredients in a food processor or blender. Serve as a filling for tomato aspic ring or as a dressing for a citrus salad plate. Guacamole has been sold short as being a dip for yucky potato or corn chips. It is fabulous on pumpernickel bread to serve with chicken or seafood salad plates.

HEARTS OF PALM SALAD
Serves 6

1 Can hearts of palm
1/3 Cup olive oil
2 Tablespoons red wine garlic vinegar
1 Tablespoon dry mustard
Salt and freshly ground black pepper to taste
Mixed romaine, watercress and Bibb lettuce

Drain hearts of palm and slice ½ inch thick. Place the greens in a large bowl. Add hearts of palm, salt and pepper. Toss with remaining ingredients which have been shaken in a jar.

HOLLAND RUSK I

Serves 8

8 Holland Rusk
3 Hard-cooked eggs, grated
2 Tablespoons anchovy paste
1-2 Cups Thousand Island
   Dressing

2 Tablespoons mayonnaise
1 Can artichoke hearts
8 Slices tomato
Boston or Bibb lettuce

Spread Holland Rusk with the anchovy paste which has been mixed with the mayonnaise. Place the rusk on the lettuce and top with the tomato.

Spread open the artichoke heart on the tomato and top with the desired amount of Thousand Island Dressing. Sprinkle with grated egg.

This has been the first course at Christmas time in the Dickerson households for several generations

HOLLAND RUSK II

For each serving, on a bed of mixed lettuce, place one Holland Rusk which has been spread with anchovy paste. Layer a tomato, several slices of onions, one or two deviled eggs (stuffed side down), and an artichoke heart. Top with a generous amount of Thousand Island Dressing--enough to cover entirely.

This is a complete luncheon plate; not as elegant as Holland Rusk I, but a very elegant "soul" salad .

LAMB, CUCUMBER, AND WATERCRESS SALAD

Cold roast lamb (¼ pound per serving)
Cucumbers (¼ pound per serving)
Watercress (Boston or Bibb lettuce if not in season)
Salt and freshly ground white pepper to taste
Rosemary croutons
Red wine
Cut into julienne strips equal parts of roast lamb and peeled cucumbers. Pepper the lamb generously and marinade in red wine for at least two hours.

On a bed of watercress, layer the lamb first, then the cucumbers. Sprinkle with croutons and top with curry or mint mayonnaise.

LOBSTER OR CRAB MEAT MOUSSE

1 Cup lobster or lump crab meat
¾ Cup mayonnaise
½ Cup cream, whipped
1 Envelope unflavored gelatin
¼ Cup white wine

3 Tablespoons lemon juice
¼ Cup celery, finely chopped
Salt and freshly ground white pepper to taste
Dash cracked red pepper
Mixed greens

Marinated cucumbers sprinkled with chives. Sprinkle the gelatin over the wine. Dissolve with boiling lemon juice. Combine all ingredients except cream and season. Fold in the whipped cream, pour into an oiled ring or fish mold and chill until firm. Unmold on mixed greens and garnish with cucumbers.

ORANGE OR BERMUDA ONION SALAD

Place equal amounts of orange sections and Bermuda onion rings on a bed of mixed greens. Serve with Brandy Dressing. This is a must with any game dinner. Canned mandarin orange sections are fine to use; some prefer them.

PEAR SALAD
Serves 6

3 Large fresh pears
12 Cream cheese balls or
2 Four ounce packages cream cheese softened with mayonnaise
   and blended with
½ Cup chutney
Boston or Bibb lettuce

Do not peel pears. Cut them in half and core them. Stuff the center and place them on lettuce. Pour a scant amount of Basic Dressing over the cheese. Serve as a salad course, or for a very special lunch, after the main course with French bread and white wine. Complete the meal with chocolate mints and brandied coffee. This combination is perfect following a one-course game dinner.

PINEAPPLE CHUTNEY SALAD
Serves 6-8

1 Package peach Jello
1 Cup boiling liquid
1 Cup apricot nectar
1 Can crushed pineapple
   (reserve 3 tablespoons)

2 Tablespoons crystallized
   ginger
¼ Cup peach chutney
   (Commercial fruit chutney
   is acceptable.)
Boston or Bibb lettuce

Drain the pineapple and reserve the juice. Add enough water to measure 1 cup. Bring to a rapid boil and dissolve gelatin. Add remaining ingredients and pour into individual molds. Chill until congealed. Unmold on a bed of lettuce and top with mayonnaise which has been seasoned with the reserved pineapple juice.

Note: A nice variation is to season the mayonnaise with sherry or brandy. This is the type salad that is perfect for large buffet suppers featuring chicken breasts with wild rice, a salad, one vegetable and hot rolls. This type salad is obviously not a good first course. Its purpose is to taste good and be served neatly and with dispatch.

POTATO SALAD
Serves 6-8

6 Medium potatoes
3 Spring onions; any type,
    finely chopped
2 Hard-cooked eggs, chopped
½ Cup celery, chopped
1 ¼ Cups mayonnaise

3 Tablespoons Basic
    Dressing
Salt and freshly ground white
    pepper to taste
3 Tablespoons chopped
    parsley
Paprika

Chill boiled potatoes for several hours. Peel, dice and marinate in Basic Dressing for several hours.

Combine all ingredients and highly season with salt and pepper. Sprinkle with paprika and refrigerate in an air-tight container. This will keep well for several days.

FRENCH POTATO SALAD
Serves 6

6 Medium potatoes
¼ Cup dry white wine or
  vermouth
1 Tablespoon wine vinegar
1 Tablespoon lemon juice
6 Tablespoons olive oil

½ Cup chopped parsley,
  chives and green onions
  mixed
Paprika
Salt and freshly ground white
  pepper to taste

Boil the potatoes in their skins until just tender when pierced with
a fork. Drain, cool, peel and dice. Toss in a bowl with first the
olive oil, then the other ingredients. Serve warm or chilled.

Variation: Add 1 teaspoon dry mustard

GERMAN POTATO SALAD
Serves 6-8

10-12 New potatoes,
  unpeeled
4 Green onions and tops,
  finely chopped
6 Strips bacon, crumbled
2 Tablespoons bacon grease

1 Tablespoon flour
1 Cup cider vinegar
½ Cup sugar
Salt and freshly ground white
  pepper to taste

Keep cubed, boiled potatoes at room temperature. Make a sauce
by warming the bacon grease and stirring in the flour to make a
smooth paste. Add the sugar and then the vinegar. Increase heat
and stir until smooth. Bind the potatoes. Keep this salad at room
temperature or serve at once.

This is not a make-ahead salad. It is not a party salad. It is one
which is perfect for informal "build your own deli sandwich"
parties around the kitchen table at football game watching parties,
etc.

ROAST BEEF SALAD

Rare roast beef, ¼ pound per
  serving
Domestic Swiss cheese, ¼
  pound per serving
Boston or Bibb lettuce

Homemade croutons
Tarragon vinegar
Olive oil
Mustard mayonnaise
Freshly ground black pepper

Cut into julienne strips equal parts of roast beef and Swiss cheese.
Marinate the beef in tarragon vinegar and olive oil, sprinkle
heavily with pepper and let stand for at least two hours. On a bed
of lettuce, layer the beef firs~ then the cheese. Sprinkle with
croutons and top with mayonnaise which has been highly seasoned
with Dijon mustard. This salad is a classic.

ROAST PORK SALAD

Cold roast pork
Domestic Swiss cheese
Boston or Bibb lettuce
Orange juice, for marinade

Cream sherry, for marinade
Homemade croutons
Orange mayonnaise

Follow same proportions and directions as above Thin mayonnaise
with orange juice, adding zest. An excellent variation is to use
equal parts of pork and broiled and quartered chicken pieces.

COLD RICE SALAD
Serves 6

1 Cup wild or brown rice, or mixed
1 Can water chestnuts, sliced
¼ Cup olive oil
1 Tablespoon red wine vinegar
¼ Cup chopped parsley
¼ Cup chopped green onions
Salt and freshly ground black pepper to taste
Mayonnaise
Boston or Bibb lettuce

Cook the rice until tender and steam well. Set aside in the refrigerator to chill. Mix rice with remaining ingredients and serve on a bed of lettuce. Pass mayonnaise.

Note: Cold, thin slices of roast beef or lamb make this a luncheon item. Toss with the rice.

ROMAINE SALAD
Serves 6-8

3 Heads chilled, crisp, Romaine lettuce
½ Cup crisp croutons
6 Tablespoons garlic oil
1 Tablespoon Worcestershire sauce
2 Tablespoons salad oil
8 Tablespoons freshly grated Romanello cheese
1 Raw egg
2 Tablespoons freshly squeezed lemon juice
2 Tablespoons white wine vinegar
Salt and freshly ground black pepper to taste

In a large salad bowl, tear the lettuce into pieces and add the ingredients in the order listed. Pour the lemon juice directly over the egg. Toss from the bottom with your hands and serve at once.

The first time I had this salad was in La Jolla, California, on my honeymoon. ANYTHING would have impressed me, but this salad is definitely a memory. Follow the recipe exactly.

STUFFED ROMAINE SALAD
Serves 6-8

1 Head Romaine lettuce
1 Eight-ounce package cream cheese
1 Four-ounce package blue cheese
1 Cup mayonnaise

Soften all ingredients and mix well. Gently open lettuce leaves and stuff. Close the leaves tightly and chill. Slice vertically and serve. This salad is a hard one for accurate directions and proportions. It is not neat to prepare, but perfect when grilling meats for informal occasions.

SCALLOP SALAD
Serves 6

3 Pounds bay or sea scallops
3 Cups celery, some tops, finely chopped
½ to ¾ Cup mayonnaise
¼ Cup lemon juice
¼ Cup dry vermouth
White wine for boiling scallops

Salt and freshly ground white pepper to taste
Generous dashes cracked red pepper and paprika
Mixed greens or Boston lettuce
Paprika and lemon wedges

Boil the scallops in white wine to cover until they wrinkle. Watch them constantly as over cooking makes the scallops tough. Drain well; break the scallops with your hands and chill for several hours. Combine all ingredients and chill again for at least another hour.

This salad is to die over. It may be served in the center of mixed greens or on a firm leaf of Boston lettuce; but, it is best as a stuffing for artichokes or avocado halves. Garnish with paprika and a lemon wedge. You will receive rave reviews from your guests.

SEAFOOD SALAD
Serves 2

Use the following proportions for this salad:

1 Cup chopped shrimp, lobster, or fresh lump crab meat or
⅓ Cup of each of the above
½ Cup finely diced celery
¼ Cup mayonnaise
2 Tablespoons lemon juice
2 Tablespoons olive oil
Salt and freshly ground white pepper to taste

Generous dash cracked red pepper
Dash dry mustard and curry powder (optional)
Deviled eggs, tomato wedges, pickle and lemons for garnish
Paprika
Mixed greens

Combine all ingredients and chill. Serve in the center of a bed of lettuce surrounded by eggs, tomatoes, and a lemon wedge. Serve with cucumber sandwiches in the summer, cheese dreams in the winter for a perfect luncheon dish.

This combination is almost too good to have its taste shared with avocados, tomatoes, or artichokes as a filling. However, your guests will certainly not register a complaint if you choose the extravagant route.

HERBED SEAFOOD SALAD
Serves 6-8

1 Pound lump crab meat
1 Cup cooked lobster meat
1 Cup cooked, shelled, and deveined shrimp
1 Cup finely chopped celery
1 ½ Cups mayonnaise
3 Tablespoons chopped fresh chives

3 Tablespoons chopped fresh tarragon or
1 Tablespoon dried tarragon leaves
Salt and freshly ground white pepper to taste
Paprika
Boston lettuce

Combine all ingredients and chill for several hours. Serve in a large cup of Boston lettuce as a first course, or use as a filling for avocado, artichoke, or tomatoes. You can get by with canned crab and lobster meat, but never insult this combination with canned shrimp.

Note: As in any fresh seafood combination, a tablespoon or two of dry vermouth or white wine changes the comparative "better" to superlative "best."

SHAVED LETTUCE SALAD

Boston, Bibb, and Romaine lettuce
Water chestnuts or Jerusalem artichokes, sliced
Anchovy fillets
Croutons
Basic Dressing

Here again, there are no accurate proportions. A good rule of thumb is two to three handfuls of lettuce per serving, a handful of croutons, and two to three water chestnuts or artichokes. The uniqueness of this salad is that the lettuce is sliced very, very thinly with scissors or a meat cleaver. The lettuce should be as thin as cabbage is for slaw. I go light on the anchovies.

Serve this at small seated dinners as a first course. It takes time and the consumer pleasure is the pay-off.

MARINATED SHRIMP AND SCALLOPS

8 Marinated shrimp per serving
1 Large sea scallop per serving
Boston or Bibb lettuce. 2 handfuls per serving
Basic Dressing
Parsley

Boil, devein and peel the shrimp. Boil the scallops and marinate the seafood for several hours, preferably overnight.

At serving time, remove the seafood and toss the lettuce with just enough of the dressing to lightly coat each leaf. Arrange the shrimp on the lettuce in a circle. Stick a parsley sprig in the center of each scallop and serve as a first course.

This is a beautiful salad to look at and obviously is best to serve at a small seated dinner because of the meticulous time required for assembling.

SMOKED SALMON SALAD PLATE

Smoked Salmon (Nova)
Cream cheese (whipped)
Capers
Lemon wedges
Sliced green onions
Pumpernickel bread
Bibb lettuce

On each individual luncheon plate, arrange the lettuce evenly and top each leaf with the salmon, onions, and then the capers. Serve several lemon wedges and servings of the cream cheese. Pass the bread, either cut into halves or party size, or place it on the sides of the plate. Individual open face sandwiches are made or your guests may simply eat this combination as a salad. Yum.

SHRIMP OR SALMON MOUSSE

2 Envelopes unflavored
   gelatin
½ Cup white wine
4 Tablespoons lemon juice
1 Tablespoon Worcestershire
   sauce
1 Cup fish or chicken stock
4 Whole green onions, finely
   chopped, tops included

1 Pound canned salmon or 2
   Cups fresh or 2 Cups
   shrimp, chopped
1 Cup finely chopped celery
   or Drained, chopped
   cucumbers
1 Cup mayonnaise
1 Cup cream, whipped
Tabasco to taste
Salt and freshly ground white
   pepper to taste

Line a well-oiled fish mold with highly seasoned clarified aspic made with chicken or fish stock. This is optional and obviously more trouble and more elegant. Otherwise, proceed by putting mousse in oiled mold. If you opt to line your mold with aspic, you must set the mold in a sink of ice and tilt it continuously until it is coated with ¼ inch layer of aspic. It is worth your while.

Sprinkle the gelatin over the wine and dissolve it with boiling stock. Slightly chill. Mix the rest of the ingredients, fold in the whipped cream, and chill until set.

If you lined your mold with aspic, unmold the mousse on a bed of the remaining aspic, finely chopped. Otherwise, unmold on a bed of watercress, surround with any variation of deviled eggs topped with dill sprigs, dill seed or weed, or chopped parsley, marinated cucumber slices--whatever.

Serve with rye bread rounds as an hors d'oeuvre or as a feature at a cold-buffet summer luncheon or informal dinner party.

SHRIMP REMOULADE

8-10 Large shrimp per serving
Mixed greens, mostly Iceberg lettuce
Deviled egg halves, tomato and lemon wedges
Parsley sprigs
Romoulade Sauce, ½ to ¾ cup per serving

On each salad plate, spread an even layer of mixed greens. Here, as in the Faucon Salad, I recommend Iceberg lettuce. Place the shrimp on the lettuce in a single layer and top with Remoulade Sauce. Garnish with tomato and lemon wedges. This is not my cup of tea, but most Shrimp Remoulade plates are garnished with carrot and celery sticks and ripe or green olives. You are in the majority if you do.

This salad plate, served with French bread and sweet cream butter, is a complete luncheon.

SPINACH SALAD
Serves 6

1 ½ Pounds spinach
3 Tablespoons garlic oil or
   juice of one clove of garlic
   pressed into olive oil
1 Tablespoon lemon juice
1 Tablespoon wine vinegar

6 Strips bacon, crumbled
3 Tablespoons bacon grease
3 Hard-cooked eggs, grated
Salt and freshly ground black
   pepper to taste

Break up well-chilled spinach leaves in a bowl. Toss with oil and bacon grease. Add bacon, lemon juice and vinegar. Season with salt and pepper and toss again. Garnish evenly with grated eggs and serve at once.

Once you get on to this salad, a cheese souffle, French bread and white wine, you will repeat yourself until you are almost embarrassed. Your repeat informal luncheon guests will not be embarrassed for you!

SPINACH AND ORANGE SALAD
Serves 6

1 ½ Pounds spinach
3 Fresh orange sections or 1 Can mandarin oranges, drained
2-3 Small red onions
8 Tablespoons Basic Dressing

Wash spinach well in kosher salt water. Drain and crisp. In a large bowl, add the oranges, onion rings, salad dressing and toss. Serve at once.

This salad is perfect with lamb or pork roast

TOMATOES

Tomatoes are easily peeled by dropping them in boiling water and removing them the instant you see the very first crack in the skin. When cool enough to touch, slip off the skin, core, and drain upside down. Dribble a small amount of Basic Dressing over the tomatoes, and sprinkle dried or freshly chopped basil leaves over them. Whenever you are ready to serve a stuffed tomato, toss your choice of mixed greens with Basic Dressing and fill each one with 1/2-3/4 Cup of the following:

BACON AND ARTICHOKE HEARTS

Allow one strip of bacon and two artichoke hearts per tomato. Chop the artichoke hearts and crumble the bacon. Bind with mayonnaise.

FRESH BROCCOLI AND CAULIFLOWER

For each cup of vegetables:

1 Tablespoon mayonnaise
2 Tablespoons sour cream
1 Teaspoon dill seed
1 Teaspoon dill weed
1 Teaspoon lemon juice
Salt and freshly ground white pepper to taste

Cut broccoli and cauliflower florets into small pieces and soak in ice water and lemon juice until crisp. Bind remaining ingredients and chill well. When the tomatoes are stuffed, top with extra mayonnaise.

CHICKEN SALAD

Variation: Top Chicken Salad with crumbled bacon.

CREAM CHEESE AND CUCUMBER
Serves 2

1 Four-ounce package cream cheese
1 Medium cucumber
Mayonnaise
Freshly ground white pepper to taste

Combine grated and well-drained cucumber with mayonnaise until it is almost runny.

FROZEN FRENCH GREEN BEANS AND WATER CHESTNUTS

Approximate proportions here are one small can water chestnuts, chopped, to one package frozen green beans, cooked until barely tender. Marinate overnight in Basic Dressing.

SHRIMP, LOBSTER, OR CRABMEAT SALAD

TUNA FISH SALAD

Make Tuna Salad according to Chicken Salad recipe. Be sure to use white meat tuna and rinse the oil off well and drain well.

Note: Tomatoes stuffed with cottage cheese are not even discussed in this section because to some people, this is the "Only way, my dear!" Sometimes I welcome this unadulterated version in honor of the appearance of the first "home growns." Usually though, I season my cottage cheese highly with mayonnaise, white pepper, chopped green onions and parsley. Most serious cooks would not even consider serving a stuffed tomato unless it is in the homegrown season. This is my thinking, and when I can't stand it any longer, I carefully stuff cherry tomatoes; several per serving. The taste is almost the same.

TOMATO ASPIC WITH ARTICHOKES STUFFED
WITH ROQUEFORT CHEESE

1 Recipe tomato aspic
1 Large can artichoke hearts. drained
1 Small package Roquefort Cheese
1 Tablespoon mayonnaise
Boston or Bibb lettuce

Cream the Roquefort cheese and the mayonnaise. Open each artichoke and press the cheese inside the leaves and center. Pour a thin layer of the aspic in a ring mold, or eight individual molds, and let the aspic set in the refrigerator. Then arrange the artichoke heart evenly in the aspic, cover with the remaining aspic, and chill until set. Top with additional mayonnaise after unmolding on a bed of lettuce. If using a ring mold, fill the center with grapefruit sections and surround with avocado slices.

TOMATO ASPIC
Serves 8-10

4 Cups tomato juice
1 Onion, cut in half
4 Ribs celery and leaves, broken up
1 Teaspoon sugar
1 Bay leaf
Salt and freshly ground pepper to taste
3 Tablespoons lemon juice

1 Tablespoon Worcestershire sauce
2 ½ Tablespoons unflavored gelatin
½ Cup cold water
Boston or Bibb lettuce
Cream cheese balls or artichoke hearts cut in half

Sprinkle the gelatin over the cold water. Simmer the rest of the ingredients for at least fifteen minutes. Scoop out the vegetables and the bay leaf. Add the gelatin, stir until dissolved and chill to start setting in the refrigerator.

Rinse a ring mold or individual molds and pour a small amount of the aspic in the bottom to set. When firm, place desired filling (cream cheese balls or artichoke hearts) in the center. Cover with remaining aspic.

Unmold on serving platter, surround with lettuce, and fill the center with cottage cheese seasoned with mayonnaise and horseradish to taste, chicken salad, or seafood salad.

A huge tomato aspic serving plate may be surrounded with deviled eggs, avocado slices, marinated broccoli or cauliflower flowerets-- anything your imagination brings forth.

A tomato aspic plate, cheese dreams, and a pickup dessert make a most delicious and "one plate" luncheon treat.

TOMATO-ONION SALAD
Serves 1

2 Large slices tomato, peeled
2 Equal sized white onions, sliced
Boston or Bibb lettuce
Red wine vinegar
Olive oil
Salt and freshly ground black pepper to taste

Chill tomato and onion slices together. Sprinkle heavily with salt and pepper. Place 1 slice tomato. 1 slice onion. 1 slice tomato. and 1 slice onion on lettuce. Sprinkle with red wine vinegar and olive oil.

Serve with a charcoaled steak or broiled Maine lobster. This is the favorite combination at The Palm in New York.

VEGETABLE ASPIC
Serves 10 - 12

1 Can small, thin green beans; save juice
1 Can artichoke hearts
1 Can early June peas; save juice
2 Envelopes unflavored gelatin
2 Cups boiling juice from vegetables
¼ Cup cold water
1 Teaspoon salt
1 Teaspoon sugar
2 Tablespoons parsley, finely chopped
½ Cup combination of lemon juice, white wine vinegar and tarragon vinegar
1 ½ Teaspoons summer savory (optional)
1 Carton cottage cheese
Mayonnaise
Horseradish and freshly ground white pepper to taste
Spinach leaves

Drain the vegetables and measure the liquid. If you do not have two cups, add water or white wine. Sprinkle the gelatin on the cold water and dissolve with the boiling water. Add all ingredients except vegetables and mix. Pour a thin layer into an oiled ring mold. Individual molds may not be used this time. Chill until set.

When set, arrange the artichoke hearts, cut in half, cut side up. Arrange the vegetables evenly and pour the cooled liquid over them. When set, unmold on a bed of spinach leaves which have been lightly tossed with Basic Dressing.

Season the cottage cheese highly with horseradish, mayonnaise, and white pepper. Fill the center with the cottage cheese.

By now, you have figured out that I am not long on congealed salads; but, I must admit that this salad is delicious, uptown looking, and perfect for a buffet supper. This is no "lady luncheon" deal.

WALDORF SALAD

½ Granny Smith apple per serving, diced
Equal parts chopped celery per serving
¼ Cup chopped pecans per serving
Mayonnaise
Boston lettuce

This salad will not hold very long. It really should be made at the last minute. If you want to, mix the apples with mayonnaise and they will not turn brown if preparing them in advance. Add all ingredients and combine with enough mayonnaise to bind.

WILD RICE TURKEY SALAD
Serves 4

2 Cups wild rice
1 Cup brown rice
¼ Pound fresh mushrooms, sliced
1 Cup fresh spinach, sliced very thinly
4 Green onions and tops, sliced

8 Cherry tomatoes, halved
2 Cups diced turkey
1/3 Cup white wine
¼ Cup olive oil
Salt and freshly ground black pepper to taste
Boston lettuce

Mix all ingredients except tomatoes, toss well, and chill several hours. When ready to serve, add tomatoes, toss lightly, and serve on Boston lettuce cups.

WILD RICE SEAFOOD SALAD
Serves 4

2 Cups wild rice
2 Cups shrimp, lobster, crabmeat, or scallops or ½ cup each
½ Cup thinly sliced green onions, tops included
Mayonnaise to bind, start with ½ cup
3 Tablespoons white wine vinegar

½ Teaspoon poupon mustard
1-2 Large garlic cloves, minced
Salt and freshly ground white pepper to taste
2 Hard-cooked eggs, cut into wedges
2 Tomatoes, cut into wedges
Mixed greens

Mix all ingredients except tomatoes and eggs and chill for several hours. Serve on a bed of lettuce with tomatoes and eggs as a garnish.

Note: Marinate the tomatoes in basil leaves and chill before serving. Top the hard-cooked eggs with mayonnaise and capers for a special lunch.

SALAD BAR PARTY

Can you think of anyone institution in the restaurant business that has done more to titilate perspective patrons than the SALAD BAR? Owners of local eateries in each American city could double the line by paying for eight words in their Sunday Showcase: WE SERVE FRESH SPINACH WITH OUR SALAD BAR. Have you ever gone to a new restaurant, shared a satisfactory nod with your fellow tablemates while perusing the menu, ordered your entree with polite anticipation, and then headed for the Salad Bar as though you were the food editor of the New York Times? Bean sprouts and commercial bacon bits I will happily pass by for the next guest in line; but, one glance at a huge bowl of mostly white, tired, iceberg lettuce and I want to find the manager. Mixed greens are easier to wash and spin dry, and the combination of flavors and textures indeed separate the "men from the boys."

This is the time to pullout the stop when you make your list for items to be served at this event. This is the time for "to each his own, " and the beauty of each salad is indeed in "the eye of the beholder." I have a friend who (goodness knows what is underneath) first ladles Blue Cheese Dressing over his creation and then tops it with Thousand Island. It is delicious.

As in your Artichoke Tasting Party, label your Salad Dressings. Have your buffet going down both sides of the table in the obvious order of plates, mixed greens, your choice of ingredients, and then a good offering of good Salad Dressings.

Lastly, place your croutons and bacon bits. Take the time to make the croutons, several flavors, and to crumble fresh bacon. It is more than worth the effort. A partial list to be completed by you might include these items: cherry tomatoes or tomato quarters in season, sliced fresh mushrooms, sliced cucumbers, green pepper rings, sliced radishes and carrots, anchovy fillets, hot peppers, bean sprouts, artichoke hearts, hearts of palm, chopped celery and green onions. You may want to offer grated carrots and raisins. Consider fresh fruit and have Poppy Seed Dressing. Be careful if you offer avocado slices. Make sure they are protected with lemon juice. Cream cheese balls might even be on your list.

Unfortunately, this is one time that it is very hard to judge the correct amount of ingredients to buy. If you have trouble making a mental check list, simply try your Salad Bar Party with your family or three or four people. The main rule to always remember is that 3 to 4 handfuls of mixed greens will serve one guest. 4 to 6 tablespoons of salad dressing should be allowed.

This is one time it is better to overestimate amounts. Everyone has friends with house guests or a sick family member who would welcome a lovely salad bowl the next day. And you will be amazed at the number of seconds your guests will take. Hurry up and have this party and you will be a pace setter!

And so, when dreaming up an idea for a Summer Buffet to some on-the-way-to-something event, try a Salad Bar Party. Success is guaranteed, the effort is minimal, and personal pleasure for host and hostess will be indelible.

XXX SALAD

Here is another salad which, to my knowledge, is indigenous to Nashville. In each individual salad bowl, serve this easy to present and delicious to consume salad.

Mixed greens
1 or 2 slices pineapple
1 or 2 artichoke hearts
1 cream cheese ball
Several slices hearts of palm
Several slices avocado
XXX Dressing

Salad Dressings

BASIC DRESSING

12 Ounces olive oil
1 Ounce white wine vinegar
1 Ounce lemon juice
2 Teaspoons salt
2 Teaspoons dry mustard

20 Grinds black pepper
1 Teaspoon curry powder
  optimal
2 Cloves garlic (Remove
  after 24 hours)

Shake all ingredients well and chill. Use two tablespoons per person on mixed greens. Two generous handfuls of mixed greens per person is a general rule. Shake all ingredients well and store in a Ball jar. This is a very different taste. You may want to stay with vinaigrette.

BLUE CHEESE DRESSING

1 4-ounce package blue
  cheese
2 Cups mayonnaise
1 Tablespoon dry vermouth
4 Tablespoons buttermilk

2 Teaspoons salt
2 Tablespoons sour cream or
  cream fraiche
Freshly ground white pepper
  to taste

Cream the blue cheese with the buttermilk and blend all ingredients. This will keep for days in a Ball jar.

CUCUMBER DRESSING

½ Cup mayonnaise
½ Cup sour cream or cream
  fraiche
1 Cup grated, unpeeled,
  drained cucumber
2 Teaspoons chopped chives

2 Teaspoons chopped parsley
½ Teaspoon salt
½ Teaspoon chervil
Freshly ground white pepper
  to taste

Serve with tomato aspic, avocado mold, or seafood mousse.

GARLIC OIL

Put at least one inch of minced garlic buds into a pint crock. Fill the crock with plain oil; keep it at kitchen temperature. It will last indefinitely. Use the oil only.

HONEY AND LEMON-LIME DRESSING

½ Cup salad oil
½ Cup honey
¼ Cup lime juice
½ Teaspoon salt

¼ Teaspoon grated lemon peel
¼ Teaspoon dry mustard

Shake all ingredients well in a Ball jar and chill This dressing is delicious with any citrus salad.

Note: For variation, add one tablespoon rosemary leaves

LEMON-VERMOUTH DRESSING

1/8 Cup lemon juice
½ Cup olive oil
1/8 Cup dry vermouth
½ Cup salad oil
2 Small onions
1 Teaspoon salt

2 Teaspoons dry mustard
½ Teaspoon white pepper
1 Teaspoon paprika
1 Teaspoon Worcestershire sauce

Mix all ingredients except oil in a food processor or blender. Add the oil slowly. Store in a Ball jar. This dressing is delicious with any citrus salad. It is perfect for watercress salad.

POPPY SEED DRESSING

1 Cup olive oil
1/8 Cup cider vinegar
¾ cup sugar
2 Tablespoons honey

1 Small onion, grated
1 Teaspoon dry mustard
1 Teaspoon salt
3 Tablespoons poppy seeds

In the small bowl of an electric mixer, stir the sugar, mustard, and salt together. At low speed, add the vinegar, grated onion, and honey. Slowly add the oil at medium speed. When the dressing is thick, add the poppy seed. Store in a Ball jar.

POMEGRANATE DRESSING

Substitute four tablespoons pomegranate seeds for the poppy seeds. Fold in by hand.

REMOULADE DRESSING

Mayonnaise
Sour pickles
Capers
Poupon mustard

Parsley
Tarragon
Chervil
Tomato paste

To 2 cups mayonnaise, use approximately ½ cup pickles and capers. Add 1 tablespoon each of the remaining ingredients.

Variation: Add 1 teaspoon of anchovy paste, and 3 grated hard-cooked egg yolks or 1 grated hard-cooked egg.

SAUCE VINAIGRETTE (FRENCH DRESSING)

In my next life, believe me, I am going to major in French. The foreign language of my choice was Spanish, and I am grateful that, as a bride, knew I lived in La Hoya instead of La Jolla, California!

However, I was not so grateful, when as a guest in the summer home of a lovely French family, with whom I was trying to appear terribly continental, my host asked if "I would care for a glass?" as he held up a bottle of Dubonnét. "Why, indeed," I replied, "Du Bonnet is my favorite!"

Nowadays, everyone seems to make vinaigrette dressing with imported olive oil in expensive "save for patio candle holders" bottles. To me, vinaigrette is still good old French Dressing, as I called it in my younger years. Now, of course, I request, "Vinegar and oil, please." There simply is no basic recipe for the perfect Vinaigrette Dressing. You are the artist, the greens are your canvas, and the ingredients are yours to mix on your palette. In your favorite cookbooks, you will find any ratio from 6 parts olive oil to 2 parts vinegar or lemon juice, to 8 parts olive oil to 1 part vinegar or lemon juice.

If you absolutely have to have a recipe. try:

6 Tablespoons olive oil, imported
2 Tablespoons vinegar or lemon juice
1/8 Teaspoon salt
1/8 Teaspoon dry mustard (optional)
1/8 Teaspoon paprika (optional)
Freshly ground pepper to taste

Shake all ingredients in an air-tight jar and shake vigorously just before using. Use a maximum of 2 Tbs. dressing per large individual serving per person. Pour and toss several times, making sure there is never any dressing in the bottom of the salad bowl. Generally, two handfuls of greens will serve one person for an individual serving.

For a large tossed salad bowl, count on three handfuls. At buffets, people seem to become "politely piggy" which always pleases me . The more selective one is with his or her choice of salad dressings. the more pleasure all consumers will derive. Now. here is my rule of thumb, about which I am very snooty. As in wines. for salad use "white on white, red on dark." By this, I mean that I use white wine vinegar with a bed of lettuce for chicken salad, seafood salad, etc. I choose red wine vinegar for a bed of lettuce for roast beef salad. Generally, I use only vinegar. Lemon or lime juice is particularly good with fruit salads for example. Wine, white or red, may be used instead of vinegar. You must experiment for yourself.

I believe you will find that the very best way to serve a tossed green salad is to first add the oil and toss. Then add the vinegar and salt and pepper to lightly cover the top layer. The oil coats the lettuce; the vinegar will hold the salt and pepper. Toss and taste; add more vinegar, oil, salt and pepper. Toss and taste again. Make sure that there is never any dressing in the bottom of the salad bowl each time. Try to use a chilled bowl. Try to use chilled plates if you are having a small seated luncheon or dinner. If you are using a large wooden salad bowl for serving, and are using garlic, rub the bowl with a large bud of cut garlic first.

For salad greens, there is no rule whatsoever. Just buy the freshest variety available, wash immediately, pat dry on paper towels and refrigerate at once. I use a salad basket for spinning. I use a large covered plastic bowl for storing. Each of you will have your own method for storage. My constant combination is Bibb, Boston, leaf and no iceberg. I always include spinach leaves when the young, tender ones are available.

Watercress turns yellow and does not keep crisp as long as mixed greens. There is nothing better than a watercress salad with vinaigrette dressing. Pass dry mustard at the table. If you have watercress, use it as a garnish on a salad plate, as it tends to wilt in tossed salads. In the spring and fall, try to find a secret spot for fresh, non-commercially grown watercress. I have special permission for "picking on her property. " If I did not, I would play "Peter Rabbit, " no doubt, in the dark of night to obtain this treasure.

THOUSAND ISLAND DRESSING

1 Cup mayonnaise
¼ Cup chili sauce
2 Tablespoons green onions,
  tops included

Chopped chives
2 Tablespoons sweet relish
½ Teaspoon horseradish

Mix all ingredients well and store in refrigerator. Most recipes call for minced stuffed olives. Please omit!

XXX DRESSING

2 Cups salad oil (not olive
  oil)
¼ Cup apple cider vinegar
¾ Cup catsup
2 Teaspoons salt

½ Teaspoon white pepper
6 Tablespoons sugar
1 Small onion, grated
1 Clove garlic

Combine all ingredients in blender. This will hold in the refrigerator until the last drop, just as Basic Dressing will. For a change, serve this dressing in an avocado half.

ZEST DRESSING

1 Egg Yolk
¼ Cup lime or lemon juice
1 Cup olive oil
½ Teaspoon mustard

Lime or lemon zest
Salt and freshly ground
  pepper to taste.

In a shallow bowl, beat the egg yolk, mustard, and the lemon or lime juice well with a fork. Squeeze the lemon or lime after the zest has been grated. You may use bottled juice to measure the juice if you wish, but the more zest the better this dressing is. Start with ⅛ teaspoon salt and cover these ingredients with ground pepper. Beat in the oil very slowly, add the zest and chill until serving time. Shake well in storage jar before each use. This is a very piquant dressing, and is best on nothing but lovely fresh salad greens.

MAYONNAISE

If I did not think it would give me the vapors, I would offer a rebate on this cookbook in exchange for "mayonnaise failure." This "mayonnaise myth" is a phenomenon I will never understand. There is always mayonnaise in my refrigerator for "love gifts" or a "thank you" to a helping hand--whomever. My donees make me feel as though I were giving them gold. Now, if you do not make your own mayonnaise, do not tell anyone. Get with it now! You will never use "store-bought" mayonnaise again.

FOOD PROCESSOR MAYONNAISE

2 Cups salad oil
3 Eggs, room temperature
1 Teaspoon salt
1 Teaspoon dry mustard
½ Teaspoon white pepper

2 Tablespoons white wine vinegar
2 Tablespoons lemon juice (Please use freshly squeezed.)
Generous amount paprika

In processor container, put the eggs, 2/3 cup of the oil, and all other ingredients. Press the button and count to 50. Add the rest of the oil in a slow and steady stream while counting to 50 again. You should have perfect mayonnaise. As in all mayonnaise recipes, if you have a failure, pour it into a pitcher and start all over. Crack one egg in the food processor container and count to 10. Add your failure and hope for the best.

BASIC MAYONNAISE

6 Egg yolks
1 Whole egg
1 Teaspoon salt
2 Tablespoons white wine vinegar

1 Tablespoon lemon juice
32 Ounces mazolla
1 Teaspoon paprika
1 Tablespoon boiling water

Rinse your large electric mixer bowl in warm water and dry. Have all ingredients at room temperature. On medium high speed, beat the egg yolks, the egg, vinegar, lemon juice, paprika and salt until well blended. Add about ½ cup of oil drop by drop. Now, add the remaining oil in a very thin stream. For a little while, you will think you have failed, as it will look like a thick soup. When it begins to finally thicken, you may pour the rest of the oil in a steady stream. Beat until the desired consistency is obtained and add the boiling water. Makes 1 quart with a little extra left.

Note: Portable mixer will work just as well.

BLENDER MAYONNAISE

1 Egg
1 Cup mazolla
½ Teaspoon salt
½ Teaspoon dry mustard
¼ Teaspoon white pepper

1 Tablespoon white wine
  vinegar
1 Tablespoon lemon juice
Generous amount paprika

Put all ingredients except oil in the blender. Blend approximately 1 minute. Then add the oil in a very steady thin stream until your motor makes a strange, different noise. It will sound like quick sand. This sounds ridiculous, but this mayonnaise happens so quickly that you will not have time to peep.

Note: I have had failures with this one. Of all things, in a bowl, put 1 tablespoon poupon mustard and slowly add your failure, beating constantly with a wire whisk. You might think your failure to be better than a first try success. This reincarnation actually spells Durkees!

CELERY SEED MAYONNAISE

1 Cup mayonnaise
2 Tablespoons celery seed

Combine and serve with fresh artichokes.

CHUTNEY MAYONNAISE

1 Cup mayonnaise
½ Cup homemade chutney

Combine and serve with chicken or shrimp cutlets,
or with cold roast lamb.

CURRY MAYONNAISE

1 Cup mayonnaise
2 Teaspoons curry powder

Float a teaspoon full on cold broccoli or cucumber soup or 2
teaspoonfuls on gazpacho.

DILL MAYONNAISE

1 Cup mayonnaise
2 Tablespoons dill seed
1 Tablespoon dill weed

Combine and serve with fresh artichokes, as a spread for cucumber
sandwiches, or with cold poached salmon.

GARLIC MAYONNAISE

Press the juice of 2 garlic cloves for each cup of mayonnaise. This
is a must for any cold meat sandwich platter.

GREEN MAYONNAISE

Mayonnaise   Spinach or watercress
Chives   Chervil
Tarragon   Dill
Parsley

To 1 cup mayonnaise, add 1 tablespoon each finely chopped chives, tarragon, parsley, dill and spinach, if fresh. Add 1 teaspoon chervil and cut tarragon to 1 teaspoon, if desired.

There is no accurate recipe for Green Mayonnaise. Dump to desired taste. Do not serve cold poached salmon without this superb combination.

HORSERADISH MAYONNAISE

1 Cup mayonnaise
2 Tablespoons freshly grated horseradish or
1 Tablespoon prepared horseradish

Combine and serve with cold roast beef, grilled hamburgers, cold sliced beets, or broccoli, and cold sliced veal or chicken.

LEMON MAYONNAISE

1 Cup mayonnaise
Juice of 1 lemon

Beat the lemon juice well into the mayonnaise. Serve with fresh artichokes. Pass with any seafood or chicken salad plate. Use with cold fresh asparagus or broccoli spears.

LIME MAYONNAISE

1 Cup mayonnaise
Juice of 2 limes
Zest of 2 lemons

Combine all ingredients and serve with lamb or veal salads. Pass with any chicken or seafood salad plate.

MINT MAYONNAISE

1 Cup mayonnaise
½ Cup chopped mint leaves

Combine and serve with lamb salad.

MUSTARD MAYONNAISE

1 Cup mayonnaise
½ Cup poupon mustard

Combine well and use as a spread for any meat sandwich. This is a must for Roast Beef Salad or with sliced lamb or veal.

ORANGE MAYONNAISE

1 Cup mayonnaise
½ Cup fresh orange juice
Zest of 2 oranges

Combine all ingredients well. This is a must for pork salad. It is delicious with cold roast duck and as a spread for ham sandwiches. For variation, add 1 tablespoon crushed rosemary and use as a spread for lamb sandwiches.

SHERRY MAYONNAISE

Add cream sherry, a little at a time, to mayonnaise. Stop just before it gets runny. Use with Pork Salad, as a spread for ham sandwiches, or with Pear and Cream Cheese Salad.

WATERCRESS MAYONNAISE

1 Cup mayonnaise
½ Cup chopped watercress

Combine and serve with cold sliced roast beef, chicken, or pork. This is delicious with any citrus salad.

Note: Many esoteric cookbooks will suggest using part olive oil and part salad oil. Try this for yourself and decide. I think the taste is grand for certain salads, but it should never be your regular basic mayonnaise.

THE BASIC
WARDROBE

The following list is compiled from what I consider to be items without which one should never be. It is my "bottom line," as the cliché goes, of essentials for being ever ready to build a salad. This is a random list which is shared with you for the purpose of giving a springboard for your personal choice of basic needs.

THE REFRIGERATOR

Salad Greens
Mayonnaise
Basic Dressing
Blue Cheese Dressing
Poppy Seed Dressing
Cheddar Cheese (grated)
Swiss Cheese
Blue Cheese
Parmesan Cheese (grated)
Green Onions
Garlic
Capers
Caviar
Croutons*
Poupon Mustard
Hard-cooked Eggs
Anchovy Paste

Sour Cream
Lemon Juice (freshly
   squeezed)
Lemon Juice (bottled)
Lime Juice (bottled)
Assorted Citrus Fruits
Apples
Tomatoes
Bacon Slices (cooked)
Ham
Celery
Carrots
Radishes
Sweet Relish
Sweet/Sour Pickles
Parsley (store in an air-tight
   jar, stems down)

*Note: Croutons are best when made with day old French bread. In a cast-iron skillet, place enough cubes of trimmed bread to make one layer. Either rub the bottom of the skillet with a peeled garlic clove, or sprinkle the cubes with garlic salt. Start with ½ stick of melted butter, add the bread cubes, stir them gently and turn and toast until golden brown. When making croutons for suggested salads calling for rosemary, dill, etc., a general rule is to add 2 tablespoons finely crushed herbs to the butter for 1 skillet of bread cubes.

THE FREEZER

Cream Cheese Balls*
Cream Cheese
Croutons
Pecans, chopped
Parmesan Cheese (grated and wedges)
Swiss Cheese (grated and wedges)
Cheddar Cheese (grated)

*Note: For Cream Cheese Balls use:

1 8-ounce package cream cheese
¼ Cup mayonnaise
1 Teaspoon grated onion or ½ Teaspoon onion flakes
¼ Teaspoon paprika
5 Shakes Tabasco sauce
¼ Teaspoon Worcestershire sauce
⅛ Teaspoon garlic salt
Freshly ground white pepper to taste

Have cream cheese at room temperature and combine and mash well all ingredients with a fork. Use your food processor if you double the recipe or if you are rushed. You may want your cheese balls more or less highly seasoned so test and taste. Refrigerate until firm enough to roll into balls with your hands. Roll the cheese balls in finely minced parsley for a lovely, nutritious and appealing effect. These will freeze nicely.

THE FRUIT RIPENER

Keep assorted citrus fruit, apples, pears, tomatoes, and avocados in your fruit ripener until they are ready for use. You are in the majority if you have been putting your tomatoes in the refrigerator upon purchase. Always select very firm tomatoes, let them ripen, and then refrigerate. Never despair if you have an over-ripened avocado or two. Guacamole and Avocado Soup are awaiting.

Here are a few more…

Twenty-one years ago, I was in a body cast from my waist down, because of a very serious automobile accident. Six weeks later, my left leg broke again when I was transferring, as they say, from my wheel chair to the bed. And, on came the body cast. It gets worse... on the third day I had my second mastectomy, which got no attention, whatsoever. It was January and I had buried Buford, my best friend, my soul mate and the love of my life in August. You may wonder why I am telling you this. Do I want sympathy for something that happened twenty-one years ago? No, I just want to tell you that I had to find a new life.

I want to tell you that I had to think of something to keep my sanity, so I wrote *My Salads to You*. My body cast was my desk. I only published one thousand copies and to my total amazement, the book sold at once.

It gets even WORSE. Six months later my leg broke again at the beauty parlor. There just was not enough bone to support me. My hero and friend, Dr. Robert Snyder, then put a pin in my leg from my knee cap to my hip. After more wheel chair, then the walker for months, in 1986 I was able to walk, able to travel and able to have a new life.

Since then, I have taken more trips abroad and in this country than the law allows, and I am so very grateful. My art trips are what I live for and the new found experiences and new ways of cooking are the "sherbets" between the courses, as we call travel.

So many, many people through the years have asked me where they could buy my salad book and would I print some more. I am so flattered- so here comes a little sweetener. I thought I would tell you how I have added to my cooking techniques. I will go to Mount Olivet cooking French and Italian ways, but nothing will ever replace simple and familiar dishes. Bon appetit everyone.

My life has changed so drastically in these widow years and my salad repertoire has grown. I want to share with you a few of the changes and additions I have made and hope you will indulge me by enjoying a few ideas beyond the parameter of the salad.

What my biography does not tell you is that I love art with such emotion that you can only understand it if you travel with me, take an art history course with me or attend my lectures. Directly below this passion comes cooking. Sometimes my dinner parties almost push it to the level of *Babbette's Feast*. I adore having company. Were I Egyptian, my tomb would be filled with my art collection, tomato aspic, mayonnaise and hollandaise in the cooler.
.

Now that the post script stage is set, may I digress by telling you about James Beard and Craig Claiborne, two of my mentors before my accident? My father always told me that great people are accessible. I have talked with both of these late great chefs on the telephone during the body cast/salad book phase. They both answered the telephone and both of them were charming and helpful.

I have two new mentors now. They are Lidia Bastianich, owner of my favorite New York restaurant, Felidia and Jeff Smith. I have mastered Jeff Smith 's *The Frugal Gourmet Cooks Italian* and I am working on Lidia's *Family Table*. The late Julia Child changed my life more than any other chef. If I believed in reincarnation, I would like to come back as Julia. I wept when she died.

Please indulge me and let me take a few minutes to go back and tell you how Buford and I cooked together when he was alive. We were married in 1955 and lived in La Jolla, California. His ship, the USS Cogswell-DD651, was stationed in San Diego. As newlyweds, we relied on the *Joy of Cooking*. but I must admit to you that we started out with the cream of chicken and mushroom soup bases and quickly graduated from that stage when we set up housekeeping in Nashville when the *Gourmet Cookbooks, volumes I and II* became our Bible. These years also heralded the *Nashville Seasons*, the Junior League of Nashville cookbook, which I still think is the best Junior League cookbook in the country. The late Emme Norvell was the driving force behind this book. What a cook she was! *Mastering the Art of French Cooking* by Julia Child, *Beard on Food* by James Beard, the *New York Times*

Cookbook by Craig Claiborne and *Gourmet. volumes I and II* were read like novels and were our constant cooking companions. My memories of Buford's and my cooking together, which we did constantly, still rank among my happiest and most tender .

Before we begin with our new recipes, I want to say again how flattering it is that people have asked for a reprint and I just decided to pullout all the stops and just tell all of you some of my new cooking habits and recipes and share with you the favorite recipes of my friends.

In 1987 my fabulous trips began again when 87 best friends from Nashville went to Helli and Bobby Bransford's wedding at St. Margaret's Cathedral in London. I went a week early so that I could go to the museums every day to start my new life. I had my very first lamb shank and first taste of crème fresh in an Italian restaurant, La Fontana, on Pimlico Road. I always keep crème fresh in my refrigerator. Julia Child will tell you how to make it. However, I use a short cut. I simply put 1 tablespoon in a half pint of whipping cream, shake and leave at room temperature for eight hours. Now, my culinary world has expanded tremendously, my waistline has also and the joys of Italian and French cuisine have taken me up more notches than Emeril could. Emeril is my television hero. My love of great art equals my love of great food. I cannot paint my name, but I surely do like to cook. I can safely tell you that my happiest moments as a widow have been and will be when my refectory table is filled with my best friends, young and old, and we are enjoying fine wine and food that has been lovingly and passionately prepared.

So many things have changed since my first publication and there are so many new products on the market. Baby greens entered (I am a little tired of them and have gone back to mixed greens). We can now buy double cream, puff pastry, and every major city has freshly baked bread---the list is endless. Basically, my cooking is still the same, but the following are some additions to my repertoire.

Now, let us get started in the salad department. I'm on a real toot with this one, and I like to serve it after the main course. Then, sometimes fruit, cheese and crackers come with port and a tiny sweet treat and sometimes I skip the cheese and port and have my signature tiramisu (use Jeff Smith's recipe, doubling the cognac).

CITRUS ZEST SALAD

Mixed greens
Zest from 1 large orange, 2 lemons and 2 limes (per 4 servings)
Chopped fresh dill
Fresh lemon juice
Olive oil
Salt and cracked pepper to taste

For this salad, just cover the top of your greens with the zest and the dill before you mix. I cannot measure for salads. Look in some trusted cookbook if you have to as to the amount of oil. Mix the oil so that each piece of lettuce has some and there is none in the bottom of the bowl. Try the juice of 1/2 large lemon. Enough salt is the secret to green salads. Stop the salt only when it tastes perfect and only then. This salad is very refreshing.

Another salad that is a regular at my house is the very simple

BLEU CHEESE, WALNUT AND PEAR

Mixed lettuce
Warmed walnut pieces
Bleu cheese (I vary from Maytag to imported Stilton cheese)
Croutons
Slices of fresh pears
Vinegar and Oil
Salt and pepper to taste

Some people use Granny Smith apples and pecans instead. Twenty years ago, this was just emerging. Now it appears in many restaurants.

A few words about olive oil. After my many trips to Italy and Spain, I have become worse about becoming an olive oil snob. My firstborn grandchild, Indica, worked on an olive grove/oil producing farm in Spain. She brought a large amount to me which she had bottled herself. What a taste, I shall never forget it. The most expensive olive oil is not always the best. Look at your labels carefully, try to find one that you think is wonderful and stick with it, or try several tastes.

Let's have a word now on balsamic vinegar. While visiting Modena, Italy, I purchased my first bottle of balsamic vinegar. After the excitement died down, I realized that I only used it if a new salad idea specifically called for balsamic vinegar. I have friends who use nothing else now but balsamic vinegar, but I am sticking to my old methods of red wine vinegar for meat salads and white wine vinegar for fruit salads. It is the same as the wine rule with meat. Red with red and white with white. Stretch your habits to white pepper on white meat and you are on a real great track. Treat yourself to this one: with a medicine dropper, put several drops of balsamic vinegar on any hard Italian cheese. The taste is out of this world. Serve at the cocktail hour.

When you are serving crusty French or Italian bread, cover your bread and butter plate with olive oil, pour in the center balsamic vinegar the size of a silver dollar .When your guests sit down, each mixes his with a fork.

About my tiramisu, I do not follow the method Jeff Smith uses to assemble this. I simply layer my lady fingers in the revere bowl with all other ingredients and top with whipped creme. Some recipes call for Marsala, but I think Cognac is much better.

One of the best salads I have ever tasted in my life, my son, Bill, makes when his family and he are in Nashville. It does not look like it is going to be out of this world, but trust me it is if you are willing to take the time to prepare it. The different textures are incredible together.

BILL'S SALAD

1 c. chopped pecans
3 Tbs. butter
½ c. sugar
8 oz. mixed greens
1 bag fresh spinach
¾ c. dried cranberries (frozen
   if needed)
½ c. feta cheese
¼ Tbs. cracked black pepper

Dressing:
2 tsp. sugar
4 cloves garlic pressed
1 tsp. dried oregano
½ c. red onion chopped
½ tsp. salt
½ tsp. coarse black pepper
¼ c. red wine vinegar
1 c. parsley chopped fine
¾ c. virgin olive oil

Directions:
Melt butter and saute pecans, mix sugar and pepper in bowl. Add pecans to bowl and mix all ingredients and toss well. Top with dressing.

My daughter, Crandall, to this day reports that she has never had a better salad in her life than this one. We were in that beautiful third floor restaurant at the Musee d'Orsay a few years ago and we had a glass of wine, this salad and a crème caramel. The salad was simply lovely, beautiful crisp greens on a plate covered with shavings of Saint Nectaire cheese drizzled with vinegar and olive oil, salt and pepper. We have tried to find the cheese here in this country.

I call you beautiful size 2 people "the lettuce eaters." This next suggestion is for you. Wraps are in, easy and delicious. Get a beautiful head of iceberg or romaine lettuce, separate the larger leaves and soak in ice water. Pat dry and fill with any salad recipe of your choice. Faucon is the easiest, but chicken or shrimp salads are just as effective.

Another Dickerson tradition has always been to have standing ribs of beef, horseradish sauce, Yorkshire Pudding, old fashioned escalloped potatoes and this lovely to look at vegetable dish. Buford's mother, Estelle, put the recipe in the *Nashville Seasons*.

CARROT RING

2 ½ cups grated carrots
2 eggs, beaten lightly
1 cup cream
1 tbs. sugar
1 tsp. salt

½ tsp. pepper
½ c. blanched almonds,
   chopped
1 tbsp. melted butter

Beat eggs lightly, add cream, sugar, salt and pepper. Add carrots and almonds. Thoroughly grease ring mold and fill with carrot mixture. Pour the butter on top. Put mold in pan of water and cook at 350 degrees until set. Probably 30 minutes. I fill the center with either a whole cauliflower head or florettes topped with hollandaise and raw grated carrots. Tradition tastes so good, doesn't it?

One of my standards is Lamb Curry. I do not use a recipe, but if you need one, go to any of my "cooking Bibles" and you will soon perfect your own. It is marvelous to go to a dinner party and have lamb curry with all the condiments, but I really like this dish best served over wild rice and topped with Ann Hill's chutney. I never tasted a better chutney in my life, and it is so EASY. Keep it on hand always.

ANN HILL'S CHUTNEY

2 lemons chopped (seeds
   removed)
2 cloves garlic, chopped
6 cups apples or pears, peeled
   and chopped
2 ¼ c. brown sugar
1 ½ tsp. salt

½ lb. seedless raisins
¾ c. crystallized ginger,
   chopped or 2 tsp. ground
   ginger
¼ tsp. cayenne
2 c. cider vinegar

Cook together until fruit is transparent. Add water if necessary Place in sterilized jars and seal. Makes 2 quarts.

Now let us have a section on the Cocktail Hour. My signatures are fresh artichokes filled with homemade mayonnaise, fresh asparagus, tail-on cooked shrimp, hard cooked eggs with caviar and mushroom tarts. Sometimes I mix poached salmon with capers and serve it in a crock with crackers. What I really like to do the best is to pass these items around the circle. It is so perfect to have 8 or 10 people so you can have one topic of conversation and one or two cold items. Then, if you have invited friends for cocktails, starters, first course, or whatever you call it, then serve one hot item. This is a good and cultured signal that perhaps a lovely evening has come to an end.

Now, here is how I make cocktail sauce for shrimp.

COCKTAIL SAUCE

Here again, I cannot measure.
  Try 2 parts ketchup to 1
  part chili sauce
Dash of Worcestershire
Tabasco

Salt and freshly ground
  pepper to taste
Lemon juice to taste
Freshly grated horseradish
  (this is mandatory)

Store bought horseradish is tantamount to store bought mayonnaise. Try to keep cocktail sauce in your refrigerator at all times. You can serve a beautiful shrimp and avocado cocktail in the living room or at the table any time. Use Great Grandmother's beautiful cocktail glasses. Everyone loves elegance.

This is really fun and very tasty. Place medium to large asparagus in skillet, cover them with water, bring to a boil and immediately remove to your sink. Test for the first time one is al dente. Cool in ice water, drain and refrigerate. In the bottom of a stemmed glass, place highly seasoned mayonnaise and put the asparagus in the glass tip first. Your guests will want to be invited back soon.

Fortunately I have Grandmother Crandall's oyster plates and I love to serve caviar and eggs in them. This is an easy way and a

Russian would be disappointed. Ruth Reickl of *Gourmet* would roll her eyes, and I do know better. Go on and put fresh grated onion on the egg half, pre-squeeze the lemon juice and cover with caviar, red or black. We do not always have to be at the highest level, do we?

One evening I was enjoying the company of our beloved Bishop Herlong, his wife, Vicki, Murray and Hazel Somerville, St. George's Director of Music and Director of Nashville Boychoir, respectively, my lifelong friends, Jimmie and Betty Perkins and my young friends, Robin and David Puryear. When I served warm mushroom tarts, David said he had never tasted anything better in his entire life and wanted the recipe. There. I was caught. I had to confess in front of our Bishop that I had cheated, really cheated. I told the truth. Now, you too, will know. In a skillet, melt a half brick of Philadelphia Cream Cheese, sauté 1 package of chopped portabello mixed with some wild mushrooms, season with salt and pepper to taste and when the cheese is melted mix well, add cognac to taste.. Put this in "store bought" pastry shells and top with chopped Italian parsley and serve warm.

TURKEY, CHICKEN, AVOCADO, STILTON CHEESE, CROUTON SALAD

For each individual plate, arrange lettuce topped with desired amounts of sliced chicken, hard cooked egg quarters, croutons, crumbled stilton cheese and avocado slices. Season with salt and pepper, vinegar and oil.

HOME MADE CROUTONS

We should always keep homemade croutons in our freezer. Fill a black iron skillet with cubed homemade French or Italian bread, dice one or two garlic cloves and put enough olive oil to coat the bread as you toss it. Bake at 350 until brown.

ANOTHER VINEGRETTE DRESSING

Since the first edition of *My Salads To You*. I believe this is a better recipe.

1 c. olive oil	1 pinch sugar
1 T. Dijon mustard	Salt and freshly ground black
¼ c. red wine vinegar	pepper to taste
2 cloves garlic, minced	

If you came to dinner at my house, you will probably be served osso bucco, 3 cheese polenta, lamb shanks and risotto, or Veal Oscar, to name a few of my favorites. A really easy and successful first course is this:

Take about 4 al dente asparagus, wrap in procuitto and top with hollandaise. Nothing is more fun than having friends over for oysters on the half-shell or mussels you have steamed in butter, white wine and garlic. Have plenty of crusty bread to sop up the juice. Just put lemon juice over crab meat and you'll think you're at the Acme Oyster Bar in New Orleans. For a main course, try this. You don't get veal Oscar in most people's homes and it couldn't be easier. Wrap about 6 asparagus in a 7-inch piece of lightly sauted veal, secure with a toothpick and top with hollandaise and lump crab meat.

Now, I thought you would like some of my very favorite recipes. By now you probably know that I am a "dump cooker" and some of you have told me that my aspic and mayonnaise taste better than what they have made from my cookbook. I go much heavier with the seasoning with my mayonnaise and aspic and this is the reason for the difference in taste. My recipes are basic and I count on you to make them suit your taste. The great thing about Leonardo was that he learned his techniques from his master teachers and from those great lessons, his genius came forward. No one has ever matched it. This is what we need to do when we cook. Learn from the master chefs but let our food be distinctly our own. Remember, except for baking, all recipes are really just the foundation.

Now, here come some of my favorite recipes in no particular order.

This is a delicious Strata from my friend, Becky Wright.

STRATA

6 slices white bread, trimmed
1 lb. sausage (regular)
3 eggs beaten with:
  ¾ c. light cream
  1 ¼ c. milk

1 c. grated cheese
½ tsp. salt
1 tsp. dry mustard
1 tsp. Worcestershire

Trim bread and put in bottom of 1 ½ qt. butter pyrex. This is so wonderful for breakfast.

Lillian Dunavant serves these onions and they are delicious

VIDALIA CASSEROLE

4 c. onions
½ stick butter
12 Saltine crackers crushed
1 T. flour

1 T. butter
1 c. milk
½ c. cheddar cheese

Slice the onions thinly. Make a cream sauce, add cheese and sauté in the butter until soft. Combine and top with the crackers. Bake at 350 degrees until it bubbles.

Brett and Annie Darken make these fabulous cheese wafers

CHEESE WAFERS

½ lb. Grated gruyere cheese
¼ lb. Butter, softened
¾ C. sifted flour

¼ T. black pepper
Pinch of cayenne
Salt to taste

Preheat oven to 400 degrees. Knead all ingredients together in a bowl. Roll a small tablespoon of dough into a ball in your palm and then flatten to ¼ inch thick. Bake 10-15 minutes. Wafer should puff lightly, spread slightly, and brown. If too thin, add more flour and retest.

In my wildest dreams I never thought I would want a recipe for somebody's vegetable soup. I was totally satisfied the way I made it, even though it tasted different every time. When I had my hip replacement, Ann Parsons brought me some vegetable soup that truly was the best I have ever tasted in my life. She told me it was Emme Norvell's recipe and here it is. (I cannot believe Emme used a can of tomato soup, but I would not argue with her ghost for anything. She was the best.)

VEGETABLE SOUP

2 pkgs. Marrow bones
5 quarts water
4 lbs. Stew beef
1 bunch celery, diced
2 large onions chopped (or 1 bag frozen)
1 box frozen sliced okra
1 large can tomatoes
1 can tomato puree

1 can tomato soup
1 large bag mixed vegetables
1 turnip
1 small head cabbage chopped
4 tsp. salt
4 tsp. pepper
Celery salt

Simmer beef bones and stew meat 2 hours. Add okra, celery, onions, tomato products, seasonings. Simmer 1 hour. Add Remaining ingredients and cook until done (especially turnip), about 30 min.

Optional: you may add spaghetti. Sprinkle fresh parsley on top. Every now and then we just have to take the easy way out and here is another fabulous "cheat." It brought the house down when I first served it, and all my friends make it now.

ASPARAGUS SOUP

1 can extra long Green Giant asparagus and juice
½ brick cream cheese
1 can chicken stock
White pepper/salt to taste

Put all of this in food processor and add left-over champagne or white wine and half and half to desired amount. Top with 1 piece of chopped pickled ginger.

MUSHROOM SOUP

Julia Childs' is the best I ever tasted, but you can use this short cut recipe.

Use 2 trays of portabella mushrooms
½ brick cream cheese
1 can chicken stock
White pepper and salt to taste
Add sherry or cognac to taste

Let us have a few moments concerning your choice of wines. Personally, I completely rely on my good friends at Nashville Wine and Spirits. I simply tell Richard, Steve, Fran or Miriam what I am cooking and serving and they always seem to give me the perfect wine. I like to serve wines from Provence and Tuscany (so that I can pretend I am there) for my house wines. At my couple's New Year's dinner party, we drank King Estate Pinot Oris, and it got rave reviews. For informal fancier menus, I like to serve Ferrari Carano and for my red, I have recently served Estancia Mertage. Anne and Jake Wallace served it at son John and Ann Lacy's rehearsal dinner along with a lamb shank. It was noticeably good. Who doesn't love to "fall into the cream" and be served Dom Perignon? But, I am totally satisfied with Veuve Cliquot for my champagne.

My "Best in Show" of all is oysters on the half-shell with champagne. And speaking of "Best in Show," I have given this some very serious thought. Pre-boil and cook artichoke quarters grilled over an open wood fire swimming in garlic and olive oil which Rachel Smith, Betty Perkins and Betty Stadler and I had in Montefalco, Italy last fall. This gets a Blue Ribbon. I have tried and tried to emulate the taste and I have failed and failed. My award for my best Italian meal in America goes to Lidia at Felidia in New York City. For the first and only time in my life I had a veal fillet. Michael Zanolli and his wife, Julie, and I are still discussing this treat. Where, oh, where can we find veal fillets? I am working on it. I also had sweetbreads in Vin Santo for my first course, and of course, we all had polenta. My "Best in Show" of all that Buford and I cooked together was in *Gourmet*, Volume II, p. 522, Crepes de Fruits de Mer. We followed the recipe exactly and the memory of this Sunday lunch is crystal clear after some thirty years.

In closing I want to tell you that very often people ask me when I fell in love with art. Because of my parents, whom I thank daily through the archangels, I think the stage was set early on. I was hopelessly gone, however, when at age 22 I first saw "Primavera" at the Uffizi in Florence. Botticelli stole my heart away. I fell in love hopelessly with good food when I was 20. The background was there also. It happened to me when I was taken to Antoine's by Mr. French McKnight, the father of my Mary Baldwin roommate, Martha Huey. We entered through the side door, Mr. McKnight's private waiter greeted us and I had my first marchand de vin sauce on a medium rare fillet. The pommes soufflés pushed me over. This was a world I wanted to live in the rest of my life.

FISH STEW

1/3 lb. each of haddock, cod and grouper in large pieces (or some other white fish).
4 garlic cloves minced

1 pint cherry tomatoes cut in half
8 oz. fish stock
24 mussels
2 cups white wine

In a heavy pan, fill the bottom with olive oil. Add the garlic and the tomatoes and sauté. Add the stock and wine. Sprinkle generously with salt and white pepper and simmer. Add white fish. Add the mussels, bring stew to a boil. Lower temperature, cover the pan and steam until the mussels open (about 5 minutes). Garnish with Italian parsley and serve with crusty Italian or French bread. Close your eyes and you are on the Cote d'Azure.

We need to talk about stock. Julia Child will tell you exactly how to make your beef, chicken and fish stock. Soon you will be doing it your own way in your sleep. You simply cannot dump too many things in. Everyone really should try to keep homemade stock in the freezer at all times. Experienced cooks just know what to throw into the pot with chicken parts, beef bones or fish parts (you need to go to a seafood market to collect bones and trimmings). Remember to always save your shrimp tails when you have them, or use a few pieces of white fish. Please make your fish stock--- clam juice for a substitute is second tier.

You will not believe this, but weekly I cook ½ turkey breast in a covered casserole dish in the microwave for 40 minutes. I season the breast highly with salt, white pepper and poultry seasoning, top with carrot slices and onion halves, top with parsley and fill with water half-way up. Cook away. You will have wonderful stock and perfectly moist turkey for salad, sandwiches, whatever. For years I have kept demi glace in my refrigerator and I could never make stock any better than these products provide. Williams Sonoma has veal, chicken, beef and even game. The required amount per quarts of water plus the usual onions, carrots, celery and you have your stock.

PESTO

We all have our favorite proportions. Mine are:

1 c. basil	¾ c. olive oil
½ t. salt and pepper	¼ c. parmesan cheese
3-4 garlic cloves	

Blend all and add cheese last.

TAPENADE

If you keep Tapenade on hand for crusty bread, you will love this:

1 c. oil cured olives (kalamatos)	6 T. olive oil
½ c. capers	1 T. lemon juice
3 anchovy fillets	1 T. mustard (optional)
1 clove garlic	Black pepper to taste

Blend all and store in crock.

PARSLEY SPREAD

Here is a very good habit to acquire. Each week buy one or two bunches of Italian parsley. Remove stems and put half of your parsley in food processor Add olive oil and garlic and process. Then use as you wish for sandwiches, seasonings. Add lemon zest and serve with broiled fish, the varieties are endless. With the other part of your parsley, blend with mayonnaise and chopped garlic and the taste is fabulous on any and every meat, fish and even crusty bread. The Italians consider this a given in every kitchen.

Marilyn Gardner's Zucchini Soup cannot be topped.

ZUCCHINI SOUP

1 ½ lbs. Zucchini peeled and sliced (about 4)
⅔ c. chopped yellow onion (1 small)
¼ c. chopped green pepper (1 small)

5 chicken broth
1 c. sour cream
½ tsp. Dill weed (to taste)
salt, white pepper, Tabasco to taste

Cook zucchini, broth, pepper, onion about 30 minutes and cool. Place in food processor and blend small batches. Add sour cream to the last small batch. Season. Serve hot, cold, room temperature. This is great to always have in the freezer .

I use red onions now more than yellow onions. Give them a try.

LENTILS
(Joann Akers)

1 small bag of lentils (1 lb.)

Cover by an inch or so with water. Bring to a boil, then cut to a simmer. Pour in 1 T. olive oil. Add 5 or 6 minced garlic cloves, 4 or 5 shakes of red pepper flakes and simmer for 45 minutes. Add a teaspoon each of tumeric, cumin and Italian parsley. This is a delicious flavor.

Lentils as a vegetable are wonderful. If you want to make soup, simply add the desired amount of chicken stock to this recipe.

I keep Julia Childs' Cheese Tarts (p.647 in *The Art of French Cooking*) in my freezer all the time also. Use "store bought" graham cracker crusts. This is acceptable in my way of thinking. My garden club recently had a fit over these tarts. They all wrote down the recipe.

WILD RICE SOUP

¼ C. butter
1 medium onion, finely
  chopped
½ lb. Fresh mushrooms sliced
½ c. thinly sliced celery
½ t. curry powder
½ t. dry mustard
½ t. dried chervil
¼ t. freshly ground white
  pepper

½ c. flour
6 c. chicken broth
2 c. cooked wild rice (and
  bite sized pieces of cooked
  chicken, if desired)
2 c. light cream
½ c. dry sherry
Chopped parsley or chives

In a large saucepan melt butter over medium heat; add onion. Cook
and stir about 5 min. or until golden. Add mushrooms and celery
and cook and stir about 2-3 min. Stir in flour and seasonings,
gradually add broth, stirring constantly 5-8 min. Cook until slightly
thickened. Add rice and reduce heat. Stir in cream and sherry.
Bring to simmer, stirring occasionally. Ladle hot soup into bowls;
garnish with parsley or chives. You may add fresh oysters or
shrimp at the last minute. Makes 3 quarts. This soup is a fabulous
first course.

We have to have soul food from time to time. In the Navy, a
neighbor named Donna Allen, gave me her recipe for meat loaf.
Nothing ever took its place.

MEATLOAF

2/3 c. dry bread crumbs
1 c. milk
1 ½ Ground chuck
2 beaten eggs
¼ c. grated onion
1 t. salt

½ t. sage
Sauce:
3 T. brown sugar
¼ c. ketchup
¼ t. nutmeg
1 t. dry mustard

Soak bread crumbs in milk, add meat, eggs, onion and seasonings. Mix well. Cover with sauce and top with 3 slices of bacon. Bake 350 oven for 45 min. to 1 hr.

Here is Ruth Rose's famous chili recipe.

CHILI

2 lbs. Beef	Large tomatoes
4 c. water	1 T paprika
2 onions	½ t. salt
2 cloves garlic	4 cans Boone County chili
6 T. chili powder	beans

Brown meat, pour off fat, add all ingredients and cook overnight at 225 degrees.

When I was visiting Neil and John Bransford in Stuart, Florida, I was served Zabaglione tableside for the first time in my life. The head waiter graciously gave me this recipe. This is really fun to make at table for a small dinner party using a fondue pot.

ZABAGLIONE

6 large egg yolks
2/3 c. sugar
¾ c dry Marsala wine.

Fill the base of a double boiler with ½ inch water and put over medium heat. In top of double boiler, whisk together egg yolks and sugar until pale and thick. This will take about 3 minutes of vigorous whisking.

When water comes to a simmer, whisk the Marsala into the eggs and set the top pan over the simmering base. Continue whisking, scraping the entire base of the pan as you go. The zabaglione will become fluffy and foam and will begin to gain in volume. Remove from heat and continue whisking so it doesn't overcook. Return to heat if you need to. It is done when it clings to a spoon like a loose pudding. Spoon into 4 small glass dishes or low stemmed glasses. Serve warm or chilled, with a dish of biscotti. In the summer this is exquisite over fresh berries.

Here is my Onion Soup recipe.

ONION SOUP

5 cups thinly sliced yellow (or try red for a change) onions
2 quarts beef stock or 1 qt. beef and 1 qt. chicken stock
1 tsp. sugar
Poupon mustard to cover
Brown flour to cover
white wine or cognac (I prefer cognac) to taste.

Brown the onions in butter and olive oil after sprinkling with the sugar. Lightly coat with poupon mustard and really coat with brown flour. After a good stir, add your stock and seasonings and simmer at least 2 hours. Float a toasted piece of French bread which has been sprinkled with Parmesan Reggiano if you wish. I do not go to the trouble of broiling a cheese covering.

Here is what I suggest for Beef Bourguignonne. It is now Becky Davidson' s signature dish.

BEEF BOURGUIGNONNE
SERVES 10

1 ½ c. all purpose flour
5 lb. beef stew meat, cut into
  1 in. pieces
Salt and pepper to taste
½ c. extra-virgin olive oil
5 thick bacon slices, cut into
  1 in. pieces
5 large carrots, peeled, cut
  into ½ in. pieces
2 yellow onions, sliced ¼ in.
  thick
5 cloves garlic, chopped

2 bay leaves
6 fresh thyme springs
6 fresh flat-leaf parsley
  springs
1 lb. button mushrooms,
  halved
1 bottle Pinot Noir
1 T beef demi-glace
Steamed baby red potatoes,
  tossed with butter and
  chopped parsley for serving

Place flour in a large bowl. Season beef with salt and pepper; add to flour and stir to coat evenly. Transfer to a plate, shaking off excess flour.

In a large saute pan over medium-high heat, warm oil. Brown beef in batches on all sides 5-7 minutes. Transfer to a slow cooker. Add bacon, carrots, onions and garlic to pan; cook stirring occasionally, until tender, about 10 minutes. Transfer to slow cooker along with bay leaves, thyme, parsley and mushrooms. Off the heat, pour wine into sauté pan; set over medium-high heat. Whisk in demi-glace; bring to a boil stirring to scrape up browned bits. Add to slow cooker, cover and cook until meat is fork tender: 6 hours on high or 8 hours on low. Discard bay leaves. Serve alongside steamed potatoes.

My art and cooking twin, Susan Pritchett Allison, came to our house for dinner with Franklin Jarman when she was eighteen. Buford and I were thirty-three and thirty-four. She experienced tournedos of beef for the first time. She still tells me she crossed over to the good food way of life with the first bite. We picked our friendship back up when I moved to Royal Oaks in 1984. When we come home from trips we report every single item we enjoyed. This elegant dish is so easy.

BEEF TOURNEDOS

For each tournedo, cook the biggest fresh artichoke you can and reserve the bottom. Enjoy the leaves yourself. Top the bottom with a fillet cooked (hopefully medium rare) and top with Sauce Bearnaise which you may keep in the freezer. Hollandaise and Bearnaise should be served warm, not hot. The sauce could break.

For years I have taken small groups of my young friends to Chicago to the Art Institute for day trips. I have always called them my H.O. T .S. because they are the Hope of Tomorrow in art and music. My HOTS are in their late forties now, and we have several large gatherings a year at a museum or other field trip of interest. Anyone can be a HOT. All she has to do is support cultural events. Several years ago, another art and cooking twin, Elena Graves, wanted a cooking class. Watching a mayonnaise demonstration is really the way to learn to be at ease with this sometimes tricky process. This is exactly what we did.

MAYONNAISE

Break 3 jumbo eggs into the food processor
Pour in Mazola oil the depth of your baby finger nail
Add 3 ~~TBS~~ salt and dry mustard *1 tsp each*
Make a circle of paprika and white pepper
Add a few shakes of red pepper flakes
3 TBS lemon juice (the frozen is alright, but real juice puts you over the top)

Start the motor and add in a big, steady stream the Mazola oil until the music of the motor changes. You are almost there now. Add Mazola until it is to the top of blade knob on your food processor.

Then add 3 more T. lemon juice. This method should never fail. If it does, please telephone. I cannot bear for any of you good readers to use store bought mayonnaise on ANYTHING.

Betsy Caldwell says the classes changed her life. She now takes mayonnaise and aspic to older friends.

SKILLET HOLLANDAISE

I have never seen the same ingredients or measurements for hollandaise sauce anywhere. Here is what I demonstrated in our classes.

2 sticks sweet cream butter
7 jumbo egg yolks (freeze the whites -some of your friends might make egg white omelets now and a FEW people still make meringues).
Try 1 tsp. salt and a few shakes of red pepper flakes.
Melt the butter and let it cool.
Beat egg yolks and add them to the butter. (A copper skillet is the best kind to use.)

Turn the stove to between medium and low and stir in a circle constantly until you feel a slight thickening. When you can see the bottom of the skillet and a "road" holds, quickly remove the skillet from the heat. If you have a disaster and it curdles, stir in 3 ice cubes and cross your fingers. Season with fresh lemon juice to taste. I use at least 1 T. Did you know that hollandaise sauce freezes nicely? Now you can always be ready for company.

Also, we did not have to go to a complicated process for

BEARNAISE SAUCE

In a saucepan, boil 2 TBS chopped fresh tarragon
1 TBSP. minced shallots
1 TBSP finely chopped Italian parsley
½ cup white wine.

Reduce this mixture to 2 Tbsp and you have Bearnaise when you add the reduction to your hollandaise. I use this amount for ½ recipe of hollandaise. Some people strain the reduction. You can freeze the reduction.

Another thing we learned in our class was that every good cook should keep "brown flour" in a shaker ready to use for roux and thickening for anything you want to be brown after it has thickened. Simply put ¼ in. to ½ in.of all purpose flour in your cast iron skillet and place in a 300 degree oven for at least 2 hours. You really and truly can smell the flour when it is ready. This habit will change your cooking life.

Claire Bailey Ewing's chocolate sauce is the "best in show."

CHOCOLATE SAUCE

2 c. sugar
1 c. cocoa
A little over ½ c. cream
2 sticks butter

Boil all ingredients together for one minutes.

Let's end with a French dessert.

TARTE TATIN

Melt ½ stick of butter, add ¾ c. sugar. Stir and add 5 apples which have been peeled and sliced (I prefer Golden Delicious or Gala. Bring to a bubble and continue cooking for 15 minutes.

Cover with Pillsbury dough (totally acceptable). Bake at 375 degrees for 30 minutes. Try to use a copper pan. Susan Allison makes this all the time.

Everyone who comes to my art history lectures knows that I could go on forever about our wonderful masterpieces. I am always sad when the last slide is shown and I hate for this postscript to my cookbook to go to press because it means that I say farewell to you for the moment. If I have made your cooking life happier in any way at all, then I have done my job. And, if you enjoy this book as much as I enjoyed giving it to you, then I know I'll get the "vibes" and you will have made me extremely happy. If I tried to tell you of every fabulous meal I have had in Europe and/or in the United States, we'd have a tome! I simply must include this one.

My Big Fat Italian Dinner

The best dinner party I have ever had was in October 2002. Rachel Smith, Betty Perkins, Mary Ann Denney and I had just returned from our annual "Lady Trip." This time we had chosen Italy. We landed in Milan, went to Lake Como and Bellagio and drove to San Gimignano. Our days in the Hill Towns of Tuscany were delicious, of course, and each food experience seemed to be more exciting than the next.

When we returned, I promised that I would have a reunion dinner so we could treat their husbands to our favorite Italian dishes. Teenie Buchtel was my significant other, and we invited Emily and Bobby Kitchel to the "inner circle." I read years ago in *Gourmet* magazine to serve only peanuts at the cocktail hour if you are serving four or five courses. I followed suit and we began our Italian evening at the dining room table with the olive oil and balsamic vinegar already on the butter plates. We passed a large platter of roasted artichoke hearts (William Sonoma), large marinated onions (Wild Oats), and thinly sliced baguettes spread with the mixture of garlic, Italian parsley and olive oil which had been blended in the food processor. The taste is sensational. We got this idea from Dario Castagno, our famous Tuscan guide. Along with this antipasto platter came a long tray with spoons filled with homemade Caponata (Jeff Smith). The spoons were in alternating directions. Rachael had located wine from San Gimignano for the evening. This label is hard to find here. Next we had our zuppa course and I had made wild mushroom and chestnut soup. I used Julia Child's basic mushroom soup recipe and added the chestnut puree.

We had my all time favorite, Osso Bucco, which was served with three cheese polenta. I use Jeff Smith's general recipe changing my cheeses and amounts for the polenta and use veal demi glace from William Sonoma instead of mock veal stock. Also, I just throw in whole baby carrots, onion halves and celery stalks instead of chopping them. You just really have to find your own self in Italian cooking. You never see any of the great chefs on the Cooking Network measuring, except when they are baking.

I had my zest salad next, serving small portions because, Tiramisu was on the way. You can imagine that we had a feast. Teenie said it could have been a movie, and I enjoyed every hour of the three days it took me to cook and set the table and the two days it took me to clean up. Aren't five days worth a memory to last a lifetime?!

If you, also, have the art-travel-good food disease, you know that it is highly contagious and incurable. And, my wish for each of you is God-speed and Bon appetite. Until we meet again, I send ever so many hugs and kisses.

Acknowledgements

My biggest debt of gratitude goes to my editor, my good friend, Mary Ann Lass.

My eternal gratitude goes to everyone of you who has ever eaten at my house for bringing me such joy while we shared a meal.

The meals that I share with my children and grandchildren are, of course, the most special of all. Their love for cooking is the greatest satisfaction I could have. Thank you Bill, Craig and Crandall, your spouses and my nine grandchildren

.

INDEX

Ordering Additional Copies

To order additional copies of *My Salads To You*, please fill out the following form and mail with your payment to:

The Dickerson Group
Donia Craig Dickerson
4505 Harding Road, Apt. #166
Nashville, TN 37205

Your mailing address:

Name: _____

Address: _____

City: _____ State: _____ Zip: _____

Telephone: _____

Amount you need to enclose:

Please send _____ copies at $14.95 each   _____

Tax at 9.25% (Tennessee residents only)   _____

$4.00 S&H per book   _____

===============

Total   _____

Please allow 3 weeks for delivery.
Make checks payable to My Salads to You.